Edited by Karl Neumann, M

THE BUSINESS TRAVELER'S GUIDE TO GOOD HEALTH ON THE ROAD

The Business Traveler's Guide to Good Health on the Road, edited by
Karl Neumann, M.D., and Maury Rosenbaum

Library of Congress Cataloging-in-Publication Data

The business traveler's guide to good health on the road / edited by
Karl Neumann, M.D., and Maury Rosenbaum.
p. cm.
Includes bibliographical references and index.
ISBN 1-56561-036-9 : $12.95
1. Executives--Health and hygiene.
2. Travel--Health aspects.
I. Neumann, M.D., Karl. II. Rosenbaum, Maury.
RA777.65.B87 1994
613.6'8--dc20 93-31497
CIP

Cover Design: Emerson, Wajdowicz Studios, Inc./NYC
Research Assistant: Patricia Richter
Production Coordinator: Claire Lewis
Printed in the United States of America

Published by CHRONIMED Publishing
P.O. Box 47945
Minneapolis, MN 55447-9727

TABLE OF CONTENTS

ACKNOWLEDGMENTS

A special thank you to the scores of business, travel, and health experts whose work made this book so unique. Also to be acknowledged are the fine publications that were used as reference material. We encourage you to see the resource list on page 197 for detailed information on these publications. Finally, thanks to Pat Richter for her extraordinary research and writing efforts, and to Janet Hogge, Donna Hoel, Jeff Braun, and Charles Roy Schroeder, Ph.D., for their important contributions.

THE BUSINESS TRAVELER'S GUIDE TO GOOD HEALTH ON THE ROAD

Edited by Karl Neumann, M.D.,
and Maury Rosenbaum

INTRODUCTION

Monday morning, 6 a.m. Time to hit the road, the runway, or the depot—again.

For the business traveler, getting there isn't always half the fun. In the United States and Canada, millions of people travel regularly as part of their work. Many face heavy traffic, long waits at airports, or just endlessly boring stretches of road. Some thrive; others wilt.

Are there some things you can do to make your business travel more comfortable—more compatible with good health?

We've heard the questions often enough to become interested in exploring various answers. We've talked with experienced travelers and travel planners, health and fitness experts, over-the-road truck drivers, bus drivers, and airline attendants—everyone who might give us some clues that could help people travel well.

This book represents insights from those who have been there . . . and been there . . . and been there. They share their coping techniques, their head messages (self-talk), and their health and fitness tricks. We hope they'll work for you.

Deciding to Stay Healthy

Life on the road can be full of temptations. Your expense account sometimes permits you to eat and drink more lavishly than you ever do at home; your attendance at dinner meetings sometimes requires that you do. Your work schedule keeps you running from early morning until late at night; you find no time for exercise. But, in spite of this, the single most important thing you

One survey found that 62% of all travelers had some physical ailment while traveling during the past year, and 20% of business travelers were forced to cut the trip short as a result.

"Each year, the average American motorist drives the equivalent of two round-trips between Los Angeles and New York, almost twice as much as his European counterpart."

—Travel Holiday

need to do is to take care of yourself on the road.

There is plenty of stress in a life on the road. And yes, it's true that stress can stimulate personal productivity—up to a point. At that point, which varies from person to person, productivity begins to decline.

Maintaining peak performance on the road can be challenging because of the added stress travel imposes. Often your personal commitment to taking good care of yourself is the best decision you can make for the sake of your productivity. And that's not just good for your health, it's good for your company.

What does it mean to make a personal decision to stay healthy? It starts with paying close attention to what you are eating—and drinking. It means taking time for some healthy, stress-relieving activity, like aerobic exercise or meditation. It means being aware of the special challenges you face on the road and being prepared to handle them. It means being sure you get enough rest. And it means being prepared to handle whatever health problems crop up when you are away from home.

To help you do this, we've filled this book with tips from business travelers, health professionals, and fitness experts who have all been there—and back again.

Things To Take Along

Determining what you need to take along on your trip is obviously dependent in part on where you are going. The climate at your destination, the duration of your trip, and the destination itself are your primary considerations. The state of your health may require that you take extra medications or precautions. If you need a special diet, for example, you'll want to make sure it's available wherever you go.

If you take medication on a regular basis, take along enough to last the entire trip—and then add a few days' supply, just in case. And don't put your medications all in your suitcase. What if that bag gets lost? Carry at least an immediate supply with you, in your briefcase or carry-on luggage. If you are traveling outside the U.S., be sure to learn the generic names of your medications. You'll want to take along the prescriptions from your doctor for the medications you need. Have the doctor write the generic names on the prescriptions. They have never heard of things like Procardia® in Europe or Japan.

Also, it's not a good idea to carry your medications in unmarked vials, especially if you must carry legally prescribed narcotics or controlled substances such as tranquilizers or sleeping pills. Get a letter from your doctor verifying your need for these.

If you have diabetes and are insulin dependent, you'll undoubtedly need to take along insulin and syringes. It's a good idea to get a letter from your doctor, too, certifying your diagnosis and treatment. This is particularly so if you're traveling outside the U.S. where customs officials might need to take a look in your luggage.

Every business traveler should have a kit of personal care and medical items that is routinely tossed into the suitcase whenever you hit the road. Quantities can be adjusted for the duration of the trip and the ready availability of replacements.

Obviously, if you are going to Cleveland for three days, you won't need two dozen gauze bandages. But if you're going to Korea and you'll be gone for a few weeks, you'll want to be prepared.

Dr. Isadore Rosenfeld, in his book *Modern Prevention: The New Medicine,* offers the following list of basics. You will want to take them all if you are going on an extended overseas tour. If you are only going for a few days, you will want to adjust the list. You may want to take Dr. Rosenfeld's book along on a trip since only some of the immediate concerns you may have about taking care of a headache or a sore throat are addressed here.

When possible, however, it's best to call your doctor back home, even from overseas, if a medical concern arises.

"Your luggage is missing—What does the airline owe you until it turns up? It's a case-by-case thing, but many airlines will reimburse you for emergency purposes, and most provide compensation—usually $25 for the first 24 hours your bag is missing. (If you're headed home, you probably won't get anything.)"

—Condé Nast Traveler

Pain Killers

Aspirin or *acetaminophen* works well for lowering fever. *Ibuprofen* is a little stronger for pain. If you're going overseas, you might want to ask your doctor for some quarter- or half-grain tablets of *codeine,* just in case you find yourself in severe pain.

Stomach Sedatives

Try *Gelusil®*, *Mylanta®*, *Tums®*, *Rolaids®*, or *Maalox®* for upset stomach, heartburn, or abdominal cramping. They are all available over the counter.

Antidiarrheal Preparations

Imodium AD® or *Pepto Bismol®* are both available over the counter in either liquid or tablet form. The liquid form seems to work more quickly for most people. Pepto Bismol can turn your stool dark and leave a black coating on your tongue, but it's harmless. For more serious cases of diarrhea, see Chapter 4 on Health Concerns.

Antihistamines

In case you experience an allergic reaction to something, having antihistamines on hand is a good idea. Many are available over the counter. *Benadryl®* has been found to be effective in a variety of circumstances and seems well tolerated by most people. Be aware, however, that most antihistamines cause drowsiness, so you don't want to be facing a long drive after taking one. If you have allergies, you will want to discuss them with your doctor, and you may want to ask for a prescription for *Seldane,* which causes little or no drowsiness.

Basic Antibiotics

Tetracycline, cephalexin (Keflex®), ciprofloxacin, penicillin, or *erythromycin* are useful antibiotics to have in a travel kit. All are available only by prescription and are effective against the most common infectious organisms. Be careful with tetracycline if you are going to be spending any time in the sun, as it can cause a troublesome rash. Also, if you can't take penicillin, you probably can't take Keflex either, since these two antibiotics have cross sensitivity.

The interaction of drugs is an important health concern. Be sure to talk with your doctor or pharmacist about how antibiotics or other newly prescribed drugs may interact with any medications you are already taking.

Mild Laxatives

Metamucil® and *Senokot®* (which comes in a convenient capsule form) are both good choices. The more dynamic laxatives will force you to stay pretty close to a bathroom. Both mild forms are available without a prescription. It's interesting to note that constipation is more often a problem on the road than diarrhea. Your diet is more apt to lack fiber-rich foods, and you may not be getting as much exercise as you do at home, so bring a laxative along. It'll make you feel better. You may also want to try to eat a lot of fruit—one of the best laxatives around.

Topical Creams or Ointments

Neosporin®, *Bacitracin®*, and *Neomycin®* are all available over the counter. Choose any one since all are equally effective. *Betadine®* should also be in your kit to handle any breaks in the skin. *Cortaid®*, a mild steroid preparation also available over the counter, can be used for nonspecific itches, rashes, and insect bites. All these come in tubes or small vials, and you'll want to have one of each of the three types.

Cough Medicine

Actifed C® is an effective cough suppressant, doesn't taste too bad, and is available without a prescription. Any over-the-counter preparation that contains dextromethorphan will work, however. You'll want to choose your personal favorite.

Motion Sickness Preparation

Dramamine® tablets or *Transderm Scōp®* patches are both effective for motion sickness. The scopalomine patches have been found very useful for travelers spending long periods of time at sea. Dramamine can make you sleepy, so it's not a good idea if you're driving. Carefully follow the instructions for using Transderm patches—they can cause side effects in some people, so check them out beforehand. If you're concerned about motion sickness, ask your doctor before you leave home.

Nasal Spray

A decongestant nasal spray, such as *Afrin®* (to name only one), is an especially good idea for anyone who travels. See page 124 on nosebleeds in case you get into more serious trouble.

Decongestant

You'll want to put an effective decongestant tablet into your travel kit, too. Choose the one you used during your last head cold that worked but didn't put you to sleep. There are lots available over the counter.

Antifungal Foot Powder or Solution

Lotrimin®, *Micatin®*, or *Tinactin®* should be part of the travel kit, since the shower stalls in the hotel rooms or fitness centers you visit might not always be totally fungus free.

Swimmer's Ear

Vōsol® is used to treat swimmer's ear and should be included if you are going to be swimming, whether it's a local lake or the Great Barrier Reef off the coast of Australia.

Eyeglasses

If you wear prescription lenses, take an extra pair and a copy of your prescription. Also, for contact lens wearers, remember rewetting drops and contact lens solution for cleaning.

Moisturizing Skin Cream

You probably have a personal preference for a moisturizing cream. Dryness is often a serious problem, not just in airplanes, but in overheated hotel rooms, too.

Sunglasses, Hat, and Sunscreen

Sunglasses and sunscreen are a must for those who travel to sunny places where they have to be outside for any length of time. Choose a sunscreen with an SPF (sun protection factor) of 15 at a minimum. SPF 30 is recommended as protection against deep skin damage from the sun's radiation. And use a sunscreen that not only screens out ultraviolet B (UVB) rays but also ultraviolet A (UVA) rays. Both rays damage the skin and will eventually cause cancer.

Band Aids

Take a reasonable supply of various sizes.

Gauze Bandages

Very important for emergencies.

Adhesive Tape

For those gauze bandages. One roll should be in the kit.

Scissors, Tweezers, or Pocket Knife

You never know when you're going to need various tools, so be prepared.

Thermometer

This needs no explanation and might be important to you if you run a fever during a road trip.

Contraceptives

Finally, for the sexually active female, condoms, birth-control device, pills, or spermicidal jelly should be part of your kit. For the sexually active male, remember condoms. If you are traveling someplace where AIDS is prevalent or if you choose to participate in any behaviors that put you at risk, you'll want to learn to take special precautions.

Rosenfeld, Isadore, M.D.; Modern Prevention: The New Medicine; Linden Press/Simon and Schuster; New York: 1986.

Special Devices

That's it for the personal care and medical kit. You know about taking your razor and shaving cream, deodorant, and other toiletries. After all, you've probably been on the road before. But, there are some additional basic supplies you might want to take depending on your destination. These include an electrical adaptor plug and current converter; an electrical coil for boiling water overseas; an inflatable pillow for long airline flights; and an electronic language translator, or some other exotic device. Magellan's International Travel Corporation in Santa Barbara, CA, has an interesting catalog of travel paraphernalia. Their number is (800) 962-4943.

What Every Busines Traveler Needs To Know

Some of the information you need to know is obvious: Where will you be staying? How can you make sure your family and office can contact you while you're gone? What are you going to be doing at your destination? How long will you be gone?

Besides these immediate and obvious concerns, there are others:

- Will you be staying in modern hotels with exercise facilities? Are they in a safe part of town where you might be able to go for a walk after work?

"Men are twice as likely as women to claim that they never get lost when driving."

—Condé Nast Traveler

- Do you need to be concerned about the quality of the food or water available at your destination? For travelers to developing countries, this could be a serious concern. If you are going to a domestic urban location, you will probably be fine, but there have been cases where people who have traveled only 25 miles from home have gotten seriously sick.

- Will you be working around the clock? Is there little time in your schedule for exercise or relaxation? Plan ahead for this by packing a convenient exercise tool that works for you. And read Chapter 2 for some exercises that you can do anywhere.

- Will you be exposed to extremes of heat or cold, or will you be in a high altitude location? You will want to be prepared to handle heatstroke, head colds, or altitude sickness if you are. (See Chapter 4, Health Concerns, for specifics.)

- Will you be going to a politically unstable country? Do you need to be concerned for your personal safety or about crime?

- Are you planning to rent a car? Be aware that auto accidents are the most serious health risk to the traveler (especially right after a long flight). Research shows that many road accidents involving travelers are due to loss of driver control caused by fatigue, alcohol, or unfamiliar road conditions.

- What recreational equipment will you need should you have time for fun? Do you need to take swim wear, golf clubs, tennis racquet, or dive gear? Remember that another serious health risk for travelers is drowning. Swimming in unprotected and unfamiliar waters can be dangerous.

- If you have personal health concerns, you'll want to know how to get medical help while you're out of town. Your doctor probably can help you with this, but for more specific information about what immunizations you need for travel to foreign countries and for the locations of U.S. Embassy offices where you can get help, you'll want to contact the U.S. State Department and the Centers for Disease Control and Prevention. Specific phone numbers and related information are listed in Chapter 4.

Beyond this, we think you need to know just about everything in this handy book. So, we'll be covering it chapter by chapter, starting with tips for how and where to eat right. Then comes how, where, and when to exercise; what to do to relieve stress; health and safety on the road; tips for women travelers; tips for men, and what to do when you need help. And in the back section of the book, there's a list of hotels with fitness facilities in major cities around the U.S. and in Canada.

"The average American spends 5 years waiting in lines."

—In An Average Lifetime

1

YOU ARE WHAT YOU EAT

Whether traveling or not, we make food choices every day. Choosing to eat right is about the most important daily decision we confront.

That old adage "You are what you eat" is pretty much fact. If you choose to have three martinis at lunch instead of something nutritious, you can rest assured that your productivity will suffer, along with your liver and most of your other vital organs.

The temptation to use alcohol to relax on the road is strong, but the potential for disaster increases exponentially when you do. Likewise, you may be tempted to use the fast-food services to handle your meals, particularly if you are eating alone. This is not a good idea on a daily basis. However, if you do eat fast food, we'll show you how to make healthier choices.

Basic Guidelines

Hope Warshaw, a registered dietitian, offers six basic skills you'll want to develop for healthier dining out. These include: (1) monitoring the frequency of eating out; (2) choosing the restaurant carefully; (3) making wise menu selections; (4) monitoring your fat intake; (5) making special requests; and (6) practicing portion control.

The more often you eat out, the more you need to closely monitor your choices and portions. If you need to watch your saturated fat, cholesterol, and sodium intake because of high blood cholesterol or heart disease, you'll want to use even more strict control over your food choices. Choosing what to eat is

---

Warshaw, Hope S., M. M.Sc., R.D., The Restaurant Companion™; Surrey Books, Chicago: 1990.

"Today the average American (8 years old and older) eats out 198 times a year—nearly four times a week."

—The Healthy Eater's Guide to Family & Chain Restaurants

If a spicy dish is hotter than expected, you might want to drink a glass of wine to put out the 'fire' in your mouth. Alcoholic beverages help dissolve chemicals in most spices.

—Traveling Healthy

easier if you are clear about your nutritional goals.

Pick your restaurants carefully. Get advice from the hotel concierge and be sure to call ahead to check it out.

Find a place that offers a range of menu choices so you can select something healthy. You also want a place where the chef will work with you to prepare a selection the way you want it, without that gravy or sauce, or broiled instead of fried. Ask if they will omit some of the salt if you need them to. Most restaurants are aware that diners are concerned about what they eat so they are willing to grant reasonable requests.

Try To Eat Three Meals

One of the most important keys to staying in good health on the road is taking the time to eat three regularly scheduled nutritious meals each day.

Exactly what makes a nutritious meal? Nutrition experts tell us we should try to eat a variety of foods in moderate portions, with no more than 30 percent of the daily calories from fat and no more than 3,300 milligrams of sodium (assuming we are relatively healthy). Also, we are told to eat plenty of high fiber food and to avoid high-sugar foods.

Nutrition researchers working for the U.S. Department of Agriculture during the 1980s put together what is known as the "Food Pyramid" as a guide to daily food choices. This pyramid illustrates clearly and simply the proper proportion of the various foods in a healthy diet. Notice how the fat and sugar are distributed throughout all the food groups (these are represented by small circles and triangles).

FOOD GUIDE PYRAMID
A GUIDE TO DAILY CHOICES
KEY
Fat (naturally occurring and added)
Sugars (added)
These symbols show that fat and added sugars come mostly from fats, oils, and sweets, but can be part of or added to foods from the other food groups as well.
Fats, Oils, & Sweets
USE SPARINGLY
Milk, Yogurt, & Cheese Group
2-3 SERVINGS
Meat, Poultry, Fish, Dry Beans, Eggs, & Nuts Group
2-3 SERVINGS
Vegetable Group
3-5 SERVINGS
Fruit Group
2-4 SERVINGS
Bread, Cereal, Rice, & Pasta Group
6-11 SERVINGS
SOURCE: U.S. Department of Agriculture/U.S. Department of Health and Human Services

The key word on the food pyramid is "SERVING." The serving size is significant because it's almost always different than the portion you're given when you eat out. Here are some guidelines:

WHAT COUNTS AS A SERVING?

FOOD GROUPS

BREAD, CEREAL, RICE, AND PASTA

1 slice of bread	1 ounce of ready-to-eat cereal	1/2 cup of cooked cereal, rice, or pasta

VEGETABLE

1 cup of raw leafy vegetables	1/2 cup of other vegetables, cooked or chopped raw	3/4 cup of vegetable juice

FRUIT

1 medium apple, banana, orange	1/2 cup of chopped, cooked, or canned fruit	3/4 cup of fruit juice

MILK, YOGURT, AND CHEESE

1 cup of milk or yogurt	1 1/2 ounces of natural cheese	2 ounces of processed cheese

MEAT, POULTRY, FISH, DRY BEANS, EGGS, AND NUTS

2 to 3 ounces of cooked lean meat, poultry, or fish	1/2 cup of cooked dry beans, 1 egg, or 2 tablespoons of peanut butter count as 1 ounce of lean meat	

WHAT ABOUT FAT?

According to the latest nutrition information, the fat in foods is a major culprit when it comes to making people fat. These guidelines show you about how much fat is found in the most common foods.

	Servings	Grams of Fat
BREAD, CEREAL, RICE, AND PASTA GROUP		
EAT 6 TO 11 SERVINGS DAILY		
Bread, 1 slice	1	1
Hamburger roll, bagel, English muffin, 1	2	2
Tortilla, 1	1	3
Rice, pasta, cooked, 1/2 cup	1	Trace
Plain crackers, small, 3-4	1	3
Breakfast cereal, 1 oz	1	*
Pancakes, 4" diameter, 2	2	3
Croissant, 1 large (2 oz)	2	12
Doughnut, 1 medium (2 oz)	2	11
Danish, 1 medium (2 oz)	2	13
Cake, frosted, 1/16 average	1	13
Cookies, 2 medium	1	4
Pie, fruit, 2-crust, 1/6 8" pie	2	19
VEGETABLE GROUP		
EAT 3 TO 5 SERVINGS DAILY		
Vegetables, cooked, 1/2 cup	1	Trace
Vegetables, leafy, raw, 1 cup	1	Trace
Vegetables, nonleafy, raw, chopped, 1/2 cup	1	Trace
Potatoes, scalloped, 1/2 cup	1	4
Potato salad, 1/2 cup	1	8
French fries, 10	1	8

**Check product label.*

	Servings	Grams of Fat
FRUIT GROUP		
EAT 2 TO 4 SERVINGS DAILY		
Whole fruit: medium apple, orange, banana	1	Trace
Fruit, raw or canned, 1/2 cup	1	Trace
Fruit juice, unsweetened, 3/4 cup	1	Trace
Avocado, 1/4 whole	1	9
MILK, YOGURT, AND CHEESE GROUP		
EAT 2 TO 3 SERVINGS DAILY		
Skim milk, 1 cup	1	Trace
Nonfat yogurt, plain, 8 oz	1	Trace
Low-fat milk, 2 percent, 1 cup	1	5
Whole milk, 1 cup	1	8
Chocolate milk, 1 percent, 1 cup	1	5
Low-fat yogurt, plain, 8 oz	1	4
Low-fat yogurt, fruit, 8 oz	1	3
Natural cheddar cheese, 1 1/2 oz	1	14
Process cheese, 2 oz	1	18
Mozzarella, part skim 1 1/2 oz	1	7
Ricotta, part skim, 1/2 cup	1	10
Cottage cheese, 4 percent fat, 1/2 cup	1/4	5
Ice cream, 1/2 cup	1/3	7
Ice milk, 1/2 cup	1/3	3
Frozen yogurt, 1/2 cup	1/2	2

	Servings	Grams of Fat
MEAT, POULTRY, FISH, DRY BEANS, EGGS, AND NUTS GROUP		
EAT 5 TO 7 OZ DAILY		
Lean meat, poultry, fish, cooked	3 oz*	6
Ground beef, lean, cooked	3 oz*	16
Chicken, with skin fried	3 oz*	13
Bologna, 2 slices	1 oz*	16
Egg, 1	1 oz*	5
Dry beans and peas, cooked, 1/2 cup	1 oz*	Trace
Peanut butter, 2 Tbsp	1 oz*	16
Nuts, 1/3 cup	1 oz*	22

* *Ounces of lean meat these items count as*

FATS, OILS, AND SWEETS

USE SPARINGLY

Butter, margarine, 1 tsp	—	4
Mayonnaise, 1 Tbsp	—	11
Salad dressing, 1 Tbsp	—	7
Reduced-calorie salad dressing, 1 Tbsp	—	*
Sour cream, 2 Tbsp	—	6
Cream cheese, 1 oz	—	10
Sugar, jam, jelly, 1 tsp	—	0
Cola, 12 oz	—	0
Fruit drink, ade, 12 oz	—	0
Chocolate bar, 1 oz	—	9
Sherbet, 1/2 cup	—	2
Fruit sorbet, 1/2 cup	—	0
Gelatin dessert, 1/2 cup	—	0

* *Check product label*

Tips to avoid the Bad Breath Blues:

1. Brush your teeth at least twice a day.
2. Avoid excess sugar, white flour, and caffeine.
3. Go easy on alcohol.
4. Don't smoke.

—Minute Health Tips

To maintain a healthy weight, (that is, one no higher than 10 percent above the desirable weight for any person's height and body frame) a typical woman should consume between 1,500 and 1,800 calories a day. For most men this number is 2,400 to 2,800 calories per day.

Women should eat meals that have between 500 and 600 calories. For men, meals should have between 800 and 900 calories.

When planning what to order, think of the food guidelines and remember, a single serving is usually smaller than that portion on your plate. Also, bear in mind your particular calorie requirements. Decide on your entree first. Learn what is included with the entree; you can then decide whether or not to have an appetizer or a salad and exactly what else to order. We offer sample menus that include some ethnic dining-out choices with nutrition breakdowns later in this chapter.

One of the most important considerations when dining out is keeping track of how much fat you are consuming. Fat is used to enhance flavor so it is usually in the most tasty foods, like cream sauces and salad dressings. Fat adds significant calories but doesn't add anything in food volume. A baked potato, for example, contains about 100 calories. Add one teaspoon of stick margarine and two tablespoons of sour cream and the potato is now 200 calories.

Fat is the most saturated form of calories you consume. A single gram of fat has 9 calories. Carbohydrate and protein foods have about half the calories of fat, measuring only 4 calories per gram each, so it is very important to recognize where fat may be hidden.

Healthy people should consume no more than 30 percent of their daily calories in the form of fat. For men this means each meal will have about 30 to 35 grams of fat; for women, each meal should have no more than 20 to 25 grams. In broad terms, this means that at each meal the percentage of calories derived from fat should be around 30 percent.

To determine the percentage of fat in your meals, total all the calories and then determine what percentage of the total calories are the fat calories.* A slice of French bread has 68 calories. A teaspoon of margarine has 45 calories. Put the margarine on the bread and you now have a meal of 113 calories. Because the margarine is 100 percent fat, the percentage of fat in the meal is 40 percent.

Watch the menus for words that give you a clue to high fat content such as "fried," "deep fried," "breaded and fried," stuffed," and so forth. Words that will tell you food is prepared in a more low-fat method include "steamed," "poached," "blackened," "grilled or mesquite-grilled," "stir-fried," and sometimes "broiled" (if the broiling isn't done in pure butter). Our Five-Day Dine Around Plan helps you choose and track the fat and calorie content of various meals.

**Smith, M.J., R.D., L.D. All American Low-Fat Meals; CHRONIMED Publishing, Inc.; Minneapolis: 1990.*

Don't be shy about making special requests when dining out. Remember you are paying for the meal and are entitled to have what you want.

When traveling on business, it's especially important to be assertive about asking for food to be prepared the way you want it. You'll be dining out frequently and it's part of your decision to remain healthy.

Ask that high-fat or high-sodium items be put on the side, or left out altogether. That might mean passing on the potato chips with a sandwich at lunch, or having the salad dressing on the side at dinner. You can also ask that the bread basket or the crackers that are on the table when you arrive be removed to minimize your temptations. The more often you ask for what you want, the easier it becomes.

Controlling how much you eat can likewise be challenging. More often than not you are going to be served more food than you need. The key word here is NEED. If you've ordered a poached salmon entree, it is more than likely that

"In 1992, according to the National Restaurant Association, Americans spent $323 billion eating out—42 percent of their food dollar."

—The Healthy Eater's Guide to Family & Chain Restaurants

Airlines are required to offer special meals, provided you place your order at least 24 hours before your flight.

the portion will be 6 or 8 ounces. However, a SERVING size for the meat group is 3 ounces. Sometimes it helps to put half the item in question off to the side or on the bread plate to remind yourself not to eat it.

Sharing entrees is another good strategy for handling portion control. Sharing is good for you and for your dining partners.

Remember to choose your restaurants and menu selections carefully, work toward having balanced daily food intake in appropriate portions, be aware of hidden fats, and be sure to ask for what you want.

A Word About Airline Dining

Airline food is notorious for being just next to inedible. In addition to being less than tasty or satisfying, it's just not very healthy. If your business travel forces you into the air for long periods, you'll want to order some special meals from the airlines. Anyone can order a special meal on most of the major domestic carriers. You don't need a medical reason, nor do you need a religious reason. All you need is a phone to call ahead.

The best choice on domestic airlines is the fruit or seafood plate. These are often better choices because they're served cold. There is less taste damage done to cold food than to hot food when it is held for a long time. Even if you're on a special meal plan for diabetes, low cholesterol, low fat, or low sodium, the fruit or seafood plate is a better choice than the other special meals offered. The other offerings include vegetarian, kosher, and children's meals. And some airlines offer Hindu, Oriental, or Muslim meals.

Airlines need at least 24-hours notice for special meals. For frequent flyers who consistently use the same travel agent, specify which meal you want when you make your call. They will list it in your profile record, just as they do your seat preference. You might have to wait until everyone else is served on the aircraft before your special meal is delivered, but that is usually not a problem. You might also have to identify yourself to the flight attendant to tell him or her that the special meal is for you.

As for beverages, drink plenty of water or fruit juices during your flight, and try to avoid alcohol. The air on planes is very dry and can cause dehydration.

Also, be aware that taking food aboard an airplane is no problem. You might want to bring your own healthy snack food so you can pass on the airline's salted peanuts. A small bag of pretzels or popcorn that you brought with you is much better than that little bag of protein bits loaded with fat and salt.

Another good idea is to have an apple in your pocket for shorter flights. While the airlines may offer you a snack, it might be something that you'd rather not eat. The virtues of the apple are many and include:

- A medium-sized apple only has about 80 calories;
- The crispness of the apple helps to keep your teeth clean;
- Apples contain vitamin A, which is good for your skin;
- Apples contain potassium, which helps keep your mineral levels in balance;
- Apples are rich in fiber, which can reduce cholesterol levels and even help prevent colon cancer;
- Apples contain pectin, which lowers cholesterol;
- Apples contain bioflavonoids, which stabilize blood vessels and can help reduce bleeding.

Alcohol is almost twice as potent at 35,000 feet as at sea level.

—Traveling Healthy

In a study of 400 frequent travelers, 68% of the men surveyed reported feeling lonely on business trips, compared with 46% of the women, according to Residence Inn by Marriott.

—Working Woman

Tips For When You Dine Alone

Dining alone when you are on the road can be very lonely. Don't throw caution to the wind and "pig out" on whatever you want just because you feel a little sorry for yourself. Now is the time to remind yourself that your health is important. Use the time alone productively.

Think of something you like to do and create an absorbing daydream that can accompany you throughout the meal. Jot some postcards to send to the folks back home. Or use the time to read this inspiring book. Don't lose sight of what you are eating, however, and pay some attention to that sensation of fullness in your body.

It may be very tempting to hit the Fast Food trail when you're alone. Lots of solo diners do. If you want to eat at a fast food restaurant, consult the listing later in this chapter to compare the healthiest offerings of each before deciding where to go. Remember the guidelines: for women, each meal should be between 500 and 600 calories; for men, each meal should be between 800 and 900 calories.

When trying to figure out how much fat is too much, consider this: 30 percent of calories from fat means no more than 60 grams of fat per day, or 20 to 25 grams per meal for women. For men, it's 90 grams of fat per day, or 30 to 35 grams per meal.

If you're going for a burger, it's a good idea to have one with only a single meat patty. A lower fat choice is to have a regular hamburger, or even two plain burgers instead of one double cheese burger with special (and often fat-laden) sauce. Cheese adds about 100 calories a slice, not to mention the fat, and you can save 150 calories if you hold the mayonnaise. Hot dogs are generally higher in fat, sodium, and calories than a single burger with lettuce and tomato.

Chicken and fish are often thought to have fewer calories and fat than red meat. They start out pretty healthy, but once they are breaded, battered, and deep fried, their normal low-fat advantages are destroyed. Choose fish and chicken only if they are roasted, unbreaded, grilled, baked, or broiled without fat. If fried is your only choice, go for the regular coating instead of the extra crispy kind. Better yet, take the skin off and lose 100 calories per chicken breast, along with most of the fat and extra salt.

As for chicken nuggets, consider this: more than 50 percent of their calories come from fat. That puts them into the same category as a Big Mac. Skip the sauce and save 50 or 60 calories.

Choosing certain types of fish over others can also save calories. Scallops and shrimp are lower in calories than fried clams.

Of the various sandwiches offered at fast food places, your best strategy is to order regular or junior sizes over the super-large models. A small roast beef, for example, has 220 calories, and the deluxe version has 526. Remember, skipping the mayonnaise topping saves at least 100 calories per tablespoon.

For lunch, sandwiches made with whole grain breads and lean meats, like roast beef, French dip, turkey breast, or lean ham are your best bets since they are lowest in fat. If you add bacon, sauces, or cheese, you also add calories and fat. Choose roast beef over burgers whenever you can, since the roast beef with no sauce has fewer calories and is leaner than hamburger. Roast beef sometimes has up to 250 calories less with as much protein and iron, but much less fat. Croissant sandwiches are high in calories, fat, and cholesterol. Choose whole grain breads or pita bread for sandwiches, and save calories and fat.

When it comes to potatoes, a plain baked one is nourishing, filling, and virtually free of fat and sodium. Of course, if you add butter, cheese, bacon, or sour cream, you add a lot of fat and calories. If you want your potato topped, 1/4 cup of cottage cheese or 1 tablespoon grated Swiss, cheddar, or Parmesan cheese makes the potato a completely nutritious meal. Or top the potato with vegetables, alone. It's the melted

Cheese adds about 100 calories a slice, not to mention the fat, and you can save 150 calories if you hold the mayonnaise.

Instant coffee contains between one-third and one-half less caffeine than regular percolated or drip brews.

cheese that adds the fat and cholesterol. If you can, always choose a plain baked potato instead of french fries. If the choice is between mashed potatoes or french fries, go for the mashed. If the choice is between french fries or fried onion rings, you need to know that the breading can make the onion rings higher in fat and calories.

If pizza is what you want, your best choice is cheese pizza. Top it with mushrooms, green peppers, and onions and you've got a tasty and pretty healthy choice. If you can, choose the thin crust pizza instead of deep dish. It's not a good idea to top your pizza with pepperoni, sausage, anchovies or extra cheese, since that can add up to 170 calories per slice, as well as extra fat. Add a salad to a pizza and you've got a nutritionally balanced meal.

As for salads, be careful of high-fat toppings, like dressing, bacon, cheese, seeds, and eggs. A salad from a salad bar can average 80 to 100 calories. Load up on lettuce and fresh vegetables, like carrots, tomatoes, and dark-green vegetables. Go easy on dressings, croutons, seeds, or eggs. Three tablespoons of regular dressing will add 200 calories. A reduced-calorie dressing will add only about 100.

Eating Mexican tacos or tostadas are good choices. In fact, of the fast food fare, they are the best calorie and nutrient picks. Go for the bean burritos, soft tacos, or other non-fried items. Even a super taco has less calories than a roast beef sandwich. Be careful with the cheese and pass on the sour cream and guacamole if you want to keep the fat and calories down. You can have all the tomatoes and salsa you can handle. Nachos are not such a good option. Bean-and cheese-covered nachos have about 700 calories per order. The bean-filled burrito is only about 300.

Of course, you'll want some kind of beverage with your meal. Shakes and soft drinks are sources of hidden fats and sugars. Save calories by drinking diet beverages, low-fat milk, fruit juice, or water, which is the best choice. Coffee or tea is usually available and fruit juices, which are high in vitamin C, are sometimes available and are a better choice than high calorie sodas or shakes.

Best Bets for Breakfast

More often than not, you'll probably be having your breakfast on the road alone. If you opt for a fast food breakfast, the best alternative is plain muffins, biscuits, toast, or pancakes without butter. Egg dishes tend to be very high in cholesterol, calories, and fat. If you want to have one, a scrambled egg with an English muffin is about 366 calories, with 17 grams of fat, and 575 milligrams of sodium. The National Cholesterol Education Program recommends that we eat no more than 300 milligrams of cholesterol daily (which is about one and a half eggs). If you do have eggs for breakfast one day, counterbalance that by cutting back on eggs the rest of the week.

Other good breakfast choices are English muffins with cottage cheese and applesauce, bran cereal with fresh fruit and low-fat or skim milk, yogurt and a banana, or an apple with peanut butter. Ordering a healthy breakfast from Room Service may be your best option, and if you can do that, here are some tips:

- Choose cereals (hot or cold). Have them with low-fat or skim milk.
- Try yogurt served over fruit. Or have some cottage cheese.
- If you choose eggs, limit yourself to one and have it poached or soft-cooked.
- Skip Danish, doughnuts, or other pastries. Instead, try muffins (bran, corn, English); toast (whole wheat, rye, raisin); or bagels. Ask for them to be served "dry" and then add small amounts of margarine or butter.

"July is National Ice Cream Month, Blueberries Month, Anti-boredom Month, National Baked Bean Month, and National Hot Dog Month."

—Travel Holiday

A final word on breakfast, if your choice is between doughnuts and coffee or nothing at all, having nothing at all is better for you. When you get up in the morning, your body is humming along on its "fasting metabolism." Your blood sugar may be a little low, but it's stable. When you toss in coffee and doughnuts, the sugar level rises significantly. This can give you a false sense of energy. As the sugar level comes down, you'll fall into that mid-morning slump. The best way to coax up your morning sugar level is with some protein or complex carbohydrates. These nutrients raise blood sugar in a calm, controlled way and preserve a nice, steady state of mind.

If you decide to eat at a fast food restaurant, here's a list of your best choices:

FAST FOOD FARE

Item	Serving Size	Calories	Fat (gm)	Cholesterol (mg)	Sodium (mg)
ARBY'S					
Junior Roast Beef	1 (3 oz)	218	9	20	345
Regular Roast Beef	1 (5.2 oz)	353	15	39	590
King Roast Beef	1 (6.7 oz)	467	19	49	765
Roasted Chicken Boneless Breast	1 (5 oz)	254	7	200	930
Chicken Salad Sandwich	1 (5.2 oz)	386	20	30	630
Tossed Salad with Low-Calorie Italian Dressing	1 (8 oz)	57	1	0	465
Baked Potato, Plain	1 (11 oz)	290	1	0	12
Superstuffed Potato Taco	1 (15 oz)	619	27	145	1065

Source of fast food information: Franz, Marion J., R.D., M.S. Fast Food Facts; CHRONIMED Publishing; Minneapolis: 1990.

Item	Serving Size	Calories	Fat (gm)	Cholesterol (mg)	Sodium (mg)
BURGER KING					
Hamburger	1	275	12	37	509
Whopper Jr.	1	322	17	41	486
Chicken Tenders	6 pieces	204	10	47	636
Chef Salad	1	180	11	120	610
Typical Salad Bar without dressing	1	28	0	0	23
Garden Salad	1	110	6	10	170
Reduced-Calorie Italian Salad Dressing	1 pkg	30	2	0	870
Bagel with Ham, Egg, Cheese	1 bagel	418	15	286	1130
JACK IN THE BOX					
Hamburger	1 (103 gm)	288	13	26	556
Side Salad	1 (111 gm)	51	3	trace	84
Reduced-Calorie French Dressing	1 pkg	80	4	0	300
Taco	1 (81 gm)	191	11	21	406
Super Taco	1 (135 gm)	288	17	37	765
Fajita Pita	1 (175 gm)	278	7	30	611
Chicken Fajita Pita	1 (189 gm)	292	8	34	703
Salsa	1 pkg	8	0	0	129
Chicken Strips	4 (125 gm)	349	14	68	748
Shrimp	10 (84 gm)	270	16	84	669
Sweet & Sour Sauce	1 pkg	40	trace	trace	160
Seafood Cocktail Sauce	1 pkg	57	trace	0	367
Orange Juice	6 oz	80	0	0	0
Breakfast Jack	1 (126 gm)	307	13	203	871

Item	Serving Size	Calories	Fat (gm)	Cholesterol (mg)	Sodium (mg)
KFC					
Original Recipe Chicken:					
Wing	1 (56 gm)	181	12	n/a	387
Side Breast	1 (95 gm)	276	17	n/a	654
Center Breast	1 (107 gm)	257	14	n/a	532
Drumstick	1 (58 gm)	147	9	n/a	269
Thigh	1 (96 gm)	278	19	n/a	517
Mashed Potatoes with Gravy	1 (86 gm)	62	1	n/a	297
Mashed Potatoes	1 (80 gm)	59	trace	n/a	228
Corn on the Cob	1 (143 gm)	176	3	n/a	21
Cole Slaw	1 (79 gm)	103	6	n/a	171
Potato Salad	1 (90 gm)	141	9	n/a	396
Baked Beans	1 (89 gm)	105	1	n/a	387
LONG JOHN SILVER'S					
Shrimp Salad with Crackers	1	183	3	n/a	658
Battered Fish a la carte	1 (3 oz)	202	12	n/a	673
Kitchen Breaded Fish a la carte	1 (2 oz)	122	5	n/a	374
Catfish Fillet a la carte	1 (2.7 oz)	203	12	n/a	469
Tender Chicken a la carte	1 (2.2 oz)	152	8	n/a	515
Battered Scallops	3 (2.1 oz)	159	9	n/a	503
Breaded Oysters	3 (2.1 oz)	180	9	n/a	195
Baked Fish with Sauce	1 (5.5 oz)	151	2	n/a	361
Clam Chowder	1 (6.6 oz)	140	6	n/a	590
Corn on the Cob	1 ear	176	4	n/a	trace
Mixed Vegetables	1 (4 oz)	60	2	n/a	330
Seafood Sauce	1 oz	34	trace	n/a	357
Tartar Sauce	1 oz	117	11	n/a	228
Reduced-Calorie Italian Dressing	1.5 oz	20	1	n/a	882

n/a = information not available.

Item	Serving Size	Calories	Fat (gm)	Cholesterol (mg)	Sodium (mg)
MCDONALD'S					
Hamburger	1 (102 gm)	257	10	37	460
Quarter Pounder	1 (166 gm)	414	21	86	660
Chicken McNuggets	6 (113 gm)	288	16	65	520
Chef Salad	1 (283 gm)	231	14	152	490
Shrimp Salad	1 (262 gm)	104	3	193	480
Chicken Oriental Salad	1 (244 gm)	141	3	78	230
Side Salad	1 (115 gm)	57	3	53	85
Lite Vinaigrette Dressing	1/2 oz	15	1	0	60
Egg McMuffin	1 (138 gm)	293	12	226	740
Scrambled Eggs	1 (100 gm)	157	11	545	290
English Muffin with Butter	1 (59 gm)	169	5	9	270
PIZZA HUT					
Thin-n-Crispy Pizza, Beef	3 slices	490	19	n/a	n/a
Thin-n-Crispy Pizza, Cheese	3 slices	450	15	n/a	n/a
Thin-n-Crispy Pizza, Supreme	3 slices	510	21	n/a	n/a
Thick 'n Chewy Pizza, Cheese	3 slices	560	14	n/a	n/a
Thick 'n Chewy Pizza, Supreme	3 slices	640	22	n/a	n/a

n/a = information not available.

Item	Serving Size	Calories	Fat (gm)	Cholesterol (mg)	Sodium (mg)
ROY ROGERS					
Small Hamburger	1	222	9	26	336
Roast Beef Sandwich	1	403	15	70	954
Chicken Breast	1	412	24	118	609
Chicken Wing	1	192	13	47	285
Thigh	1	296	20	85	406
Leg	1	140	8	40	190
Biscuit	1	231	12	<5	575
Cole Slaw	1	110	7	<5	261
Egg and Biscuit Platter	1	557	34	417	1020
Salad Bar Best Bets:					
Sliced Beets	1/4 cup	18	trace	n/a	162
Broccoli	1/4 cup	6	trace	n/a	6
Shredded Carrots	1/4 cup	12	trace	n/a	10
Cucumbers	5 - 6 slices	4	trace	n/a	2
Green Pepper	2 Tbsp	3	trace	n/a	trace
Lettuce	1 cup	7	trace	n/a	4
Green Peas	1/4 cup	28	trace	n/a	41
Tomatoes	3 slices	20	trace	n/a	3
Lo-Cal Italian Dressing	2 Tbsp	70	6	n/.a	100
SHAKEY'S PIZZA					
Thin Crust Cheese Pizza (12")	1/10	133	5	13	323
Thin Crust Onion, Green Pepper, Olive, Mushroom (12")	1/10	125	5	11	313
Thick Crust Cheese Pizza (12")	1/10	170	5	13	421
Thick Crust Onion, Green Pepper, Mushroom, Olive Pizza (12")	1/10	162	4	13	418
Homestyle Cheese Pizza (12")	1/10	303	14	21	591
Homestyle Onion, Green Pepper, Olive, Mushroom Pizza (12")	1/10	320	14	21	652

n/a = information not available.

Item	Serving Size	Calories	Fat (gm)	Cholesterol (mg)	Sodium (mg)

TACO BELL

Item	Serving Size	Calories	Fat (gm)	Cholesterol (mg)	Sodium (mg)
Bean Burrito	1 (191 gm)	359	11	13	922
Beef Burrito	1 (191 gm)	402	17	59	993
Tostada	1 (156 gm)	243	11	18	670
Beefy Tostada	1 (196 gm)	322	20	40	764
Taco	1 (78 gm)	184	11	32	274
Taco Sauce	1 pkg	2	trace	0	126
Salsa	1 (10 gm)	18	trace	0	376
Guacamole	1 (21 gm)	34	2	0	113
Pintos and Cheese	1 (127 gm)	194	10	19	733
Soft Taco	1 (92 gm)	228	12	32	516
Taco Salad with					
Salsa, without Shell	1 (530 gm)	520	31	80	1431
Fajita Steak Taco	1 (142 gm)	235	11	14	507
with Sour Cream	1 (163 gm)	281	15	14	507
with Guacamole	1 (163 gm)	269	13	14	620
Chicken Fajita	1 (135 gm)	226	10	44	619

WENDY'S

Item	Serving Size	Calories	Fat (gm)	Cholesterol (mg)	Sodium (mg)
Single Hamburger on White Bun	1 (127 gm)	350	16	75	360
Double Hamburger					
on White Bun	1 (203 gm)	560	30	150	465
Fish Fillet	1 (92 gm)	210	11	45	475
Multi-Grain Bun	1 (48 gm)	140	3	trace	215
Chicken Breast on White Bun	1 (138 gm)	340	12	60	565
Plain Baked Potato	1 (250 gm)	250	2	trace	60
Chili and Cheese Potato	1 (400 gm)	510	20	22	610
Crispy Chicken Nuggets	6 pieces	310	21	50	660
Garden Spot Salad Bar					
Iceberg Lettuce	3 cup	20	trace	0	20
Romaine Lettuce	1 cup	9	trace	0	5
Cole Slaw	1/4 cup	80	5	40	165
Cottage Cheese	1/2 cup	110	4	20	425
Turkey Ham	1/4 cup	50	2	n/a	n/a
Alfalfa Sprouts	1 oz	8	trace	0	trace

n/a = information not available.

Item	Serving Size	Calories	Fat (gm)	Cholesterol (mg)	Sodium (mg)

WENDY'S (CONT)

Item	Serving Size	Calories	Fat (gm)	Cholesterol (mg)	Sodium (mg)
Broccoli	1/2 cup	12	trace	0	5
Carrots	1/4 cup	trace	trace	0	15
Cauliflower	1/2 cup	12	trace	0	10
Celery	1 Tbsp	0	trace	0	5
Cucumbers	4 slices	2	trace	0	trace
Green Peas	1 oz	25	trace	0	35
Green Pepper	1/4 cup	3	trace	0	5
Mushrooms	1/4 cup	4	trace	0	trace
Radishes	1/2 oz	1	trace	0	trace
Tomatoes	1 oz	6	trace	0	5
Salad Dressings (1 ladle = 2 Tbsps)					
Wine Vinegar	1 Tbsp	2	trace	0	5
Reduced-Calorie Italian	1 Tbsp	25	2	0	180
Breakfast Sandwich	1 (129 gm)	370	19	200	770
Omelet, Mushroom, Green Pepper, Onion	1 (114 gm)	210	15	460	200
Scrambled Eggs	2 eggs	190	12	450	160
Orange Juice	6 oz	80	trace	0	trace
White Toast	2 slices	250	9	20	410

WHITE CASTLE

Item	Serving Size	Calories	Fat (gm)	Cholesterol (mg)	Sodium (mg)
Hamburger	1 (2 oz)	161	8	n/a	266
Fish without Tartar Sauce	1 (2.1 oz)	155	5	n/a	201
Sausage and Egg Sandwich	1 (3.4 oz)	322	22	n/a	698
Chicken Sandwich	1 (2.3 oz)	186	7	n/a	497
Onion Rings	1 (2.1 oz)	245	13	n/a	566

ZANTIGO

Item	Serving Size	Calories	Fat (gm)	Cholesterol (mg)	Sodium (mg)
Taco	1 (85 gm)	198	12	n/a	318
Taco Burrito	1 (199 gm)	415	19	n/a	815
Mild Cheese Chilito	1 (115 gm)	330	15	n/a	505
Hot Cheese Chilito	1 (115 gm)	329	15	n/a	466

n/a = information not available.

Tips For Dining With Others

There are many occasions in the life on the road when you will be having companions who dine with you at lunch or dinner. The boss calls a dinner meeting for six o'clock. The guys say, "Let's go grab a sandwich," at lunch.

You need not shy away from any of these invitations even though you've decided to choose more healthful foods.

Your best choices for lunch are sandwiches of lean meats or poultry on whole grain or pita breads with lettuce and tomato (holding the mayonnaise saves about 100 calories per tablespoon), or salads of fresh, crispy mixed greens (with dressing on the side).

If the gang decides to go for fast food, check the options carefully. If they decide to have a heavier meal at noontime, read the section later in this chapter with the suggested five-day menus.

One of the best advantages to dining with others is being able to share an entree. Remember our discussion about serving sizes and portions? Usually there are enough calories in half a sandwich to sustain you for the afternoon's activities.

If you're going for pizza, sharing is the norm. And if you're eating Chinese, you're more than likely to share, also. So sharing a sandwich in the corner deli shouldn't seem awkward.

In deciding which sandwich to eat, below is a chart that shows the fat and calorie content of some deli offerings.

Choose Smart at the Deli

Item	Fat (gms)	Calories
Salami, 2 oz	21.6	256
Bologna, 2 oz	15.6	172
Liverwurst, 2 oz	14.0	177
Summer Sausage, 2 oz	13.8	174
Broiled Ham, 2 oz	9.6	132
Turkey Roll, 2 oz	2.5	67

The Worst Breath-Killers:

5. Fish
4. Cheese
3. Cold Cuts
2. Onions
1. Garlic

"Americans bought $25.9 billion worth of candy and snacks in 1992, compared with $16.4 billion they spent on fruit."

—National Confectioners Association

You might want to skip the pickle on that deli plate, if you're watching your salt intake.

Pickles, tasty though they are, are extremely high in sodium. And don't be shy about asking that the potato chips be left off the plate when you order your sandwich.

Potato chips are one of those sources of fat and sodium that you don't really want or need. Fifteen of them makes a serving; that's only 3/4 of an ounce. An order of cole slaw or a tossed salad with dressing on the side are much better choices. They will fill you up with fewer calories and much less fat.

Here's our list of tips for planning for those times when you'll have lunch out:

---

1. Try salads with low-fat protein sources, such as turkey, chicken, fish, yogurt, or cottage cheese.

2. Sandwiches made with lean cuts of meat—turkey, chicken, ham, beef, etc.—are good choices. Avoid cold cuts and cheese. Ask for the mayonnaise to be left off or have it on the side. Try mustard, instead.

3. Salads—vegetable, cole slaw, bean salad—are good side dishes.

4. A plain grilled hamburger (quarter pound) will be a better choice than grilled cheese or frankfurter. It will also be a better choice than deep fat fried chicken and fish sandwiches.

5. Soups can also be excellent choices, but watch out for the cream-based ones.

6. Fresh fruit, fruit cup, low-fat yogurt, fruit ices, or sherbet are better dessert choices than ice cream, cakes, pies, or cookies.

Tips For Group Dinners Out

1. Cocktails and liquor can add many calories. Have liquor mixed with water, juice, low-calorie soft drinks, or club soda instead or pre-sweetened mixes. A glass of wine with club soda (a spritzer) is a good choice. Sparkling water or juice is even better. Avoid high-salt, high-fat snacks.

2. For an appetizer, try melon or other fresh fruit or fruit juices, raw vegetables, broths, shellfish, or low-calorie dip.

3. Ask for salad dressings on the side and use them sparingly. Mix your own oil and vinegar. Lemon juice and spices make an excellent low-calorie dressing.

4. Fish, poultry, lean meat, or shellfish are good choices for an entree. Have them baked, broiled, poached, steamed, stir-fried, or sauteed in small amounts of oil or margarine. Ask for a 4-ounce portion and have sauces or gravies served on the side. If you order beef, a filet mignon or shish kebob are your best choices. But, don't let them wrap that filet in bacon!

5. Choose a vegetable that is prepared without sauce or butter. Use lemon juice, vinegar, and pepper as seasonings. Limit sour cream on potatoes. Instead try unflavored yogurt or a little grated Parmesan cheese, a dash of Worcestershire sauce and pepper, or lemon and pepper.

6. Be careful of dishes containing soy sauce or monosodium glutamate (MSG)—both are high in sodium. MSG can often be left out of a dish at your request.

From: Franz, M.J., R.D., M.S.; Hedding, B.K., R.D., M.Ph.; and Leitch, G. B.S.; Opening the Door to Good Nutrition. DCI Publishing. Minneapolis: 1985.

Truck stops with best food, according to truckers:

1. Petro
2. Flying J
3. Truck Stops of America
4. UNOCAL
5. Burns Brothers/ Bingo

—Restaurant Hospitality

"It is not enough to aim, you must hit."
Italian Proverb

Of course, the very best advantage of dining out with others is being able to have a dessert to share. The best choices for dessert are fresh fruit, fruit cup, fruit ice, or sherbet. But if you choose cake, share it with a dining companion. Better yet, have just a taste of someone else's.

Tips For When You're In Control

And then there are those idyllic days on the road when you get up only when you feel rested; you have a leisurely breakfast of fresh fruit, freshly baked bran muffin, orange juice, and decaffeinated coffee delivered to your door by a smiling room service attendant; you go down to the hotel pool and swim 30 laps before you shower and head off for the day's business.

Happens real often, right? NOT.

There are very few perfect days in a life on the road. But on those occasions when you are in control of your day, not to mention your diet, here are some tips.

1. Preplan your daily eating choices per the following sample meals, adjusting the content for your personal nutritional goals:

SAMPLE BREAKFAST

Grapefruit half
Cereal with skim milk
Canadian bacon
2 slices rye toast with margarine
Decaffeinated coffee, black or with skim milk

SAMPLE LUNCH

Chicken bouillon
Sliced turkey sandwich on whole-wheat bread
Skim milk

SAMPLE DINNER

1 scotch and water
7 oz. Filet Mignon
Baked potato with 1 tsp. margarine and pepper
Tossed salad with oil and vinegar dressing
Roll and margarine
Fresh fruit cup
Decaffeinated coffee, black or with skim milk

Your total daily calorie intake on this plan is 1,915, with 34% of calories from fat.

2. Plan how much you will eat. You can make adjustments in exercise and food for the entire day when you can pre-plan. The Room Service chef will usually work with you to make portions exactly to your specifications.

3. Be assertive about what you want. You can only get exactly what you want if you ask for it. Using phrases such as "Do you think the chef would be able to...," or "I'd really appreciate it if you would..." usually get good cooperation. Cite medical reasons if appropriate.

4. Try to eat according to a schedule that enables you to have time for some exercise and relaxation.

5. Being in good control means that you are clear about your definition of fullness. Most people respond to external instead of internal cues. If you define fullness as a bloated feeling, you are likely to overeat frequently. Learn to listen to your internal signals. How does your stomach feel when you have had enough to eat? Slow down the pace of your eating to allow your body to recognize fullness. Take time to enjoy and think about what you are eating. This helps you to feel satisfied, and feeling satisfied helps you to control your portion sizes, not just when you're on the road, but anytime.

"When I went duck hunting with Bear Bryant, he shot at one but it kept flying. 'John,' he said, 'there flies a dead duck.' Now, that's confidence."
John McKay

No smoking section, please.

"The American Cancer Society estimates that more than 6,000 innocent nonsmokers die each year in the U.S. because of the inhalation of others' cigarette smoke."

—America By The Numbers

Tips For When You're Not In Control

Compulsory attendance at banquets and conventions can be the bane of the business traveler. Sometimes it seems there are more ways to fix that traditional rubber chicken than there are conventions in a year. When you are forced into a situation where you have no choice over what you eat, here's a list of helpful hints:

1. Never approach a banquet on an empty stomach. Try to eat something that is consistent with your health goals before you attend the banquet.

2. Eat only those things on the plate that are not covered with gooey gravy, sauces, or butter. If that means only the bottommost layer of carrots, then so be it. That's the only thing you should eat.

3. Look forward to the fruit cup and the salad. They are the safest offerings, and usually the salad dressing is on the table. If not, it's okay to request a salad without dressing.

4. If the entree is good old rubber chicken, take the skin off before you eat any of it. If the entree is unrecognizable, cut it up, push it around the plate, and leave it there.

5. If you are lucky enough to get a baked potato, eat it, but don't add butter and sour cream. If the potatoes are mashed, they aren't too bad either, if they aren't drowned in gravy. If they're roasted, lucky for you. If they're french fried, don't eat them.

6. When the dessert comes, you might want to excuse yourself and head for the wash room. If it's ice cream, it'll be melted and unappetizing when you get back, so you won't be tempted. If it's cake or pie, it'll be dry and unappealing. If you need a taste, try one bite. Then push the plate away. Remember, banquet food usually looks better than it tastes.

Alcohol

One of the hardest things to handle at conventions and banquets is often the alcohol. It's one of those social occasions where everyone has a drink in his or her hand. Jane Brody, in *Jane Brody's Nutrition Book,* offers this advice on the responsible use of alcohol:

1. Sip drinks slowly. Eat something before and while you drink. Avoid salty snacks, since they make you thirsty.

2. Lower the concentration of alcohol in your drink by diluting it with ice and a mixer.

3. Do not mix alcohol with other drugs or medications. Some medications simply won't work, while others can be dangerous combined with alcohol.

4. Set limits to protect your dignity and self-respect.

5. Know your capacity and stick to it. The smaller your body, the greater the effect of alcohol.

6. If you have overindulged, only time will help you sober up—about one hour per drink.

7. Don't drink and drive. The most dangerous health risk to travelers is auto accidents.

8. If you are flying for long hours, are in a high altitude location, or are suffering from jet lag, avoid alcohol.

In each of these cases, the alcohol can complicate the adjustment the body is trying to make to the new conditions, and that adds extra stress. If you choose to drink alcoholic beverages, the following two pages list the calorie content of various drinks.

"One out of every six adults is afraid to fly. That's 25 million people."

—Entrepreneur magazine

CALORIE GUIDE TO ALCOHOLIC DRINKS

Item	Serving Size	Calories per Serving
BEER		
Regular Beer	12 oz	150-175
Light Beer	12 oz	95
Extra Light Beer	12 oz	70
Near Beer (low alcohol)	12 oz	65
LIQUOR (JIGGER 1 1/2 OZ)		
Gin, Rum, Vodka, Whiskey (86 proof)	1 1/2 jigger	105
Dry Brandy or Cognac	1 jigger	75
WINE		
Red or Rose	3 1/2 oz	85
Sweet	3 1/2 oz	102
Dry White	3 1/2 oz	80
Light wine	3 1/2 oz	50
Champagne	4 oz	98
Sweet Kosher	4 oz	132
SHERRY		
Sweet sherry, port, muscatel	2 oz	94
VERMOUTH		
Dry	3 oz	105
Sweet	3 oz	141

MIXED DRINKS

(Ingredients and proportions vary, but most mixed drinks are about 4 ounces and 200 calories.)

Item	Serving Size	Calories per Serving
COCKTAILS		
Bloody Mary	10 oz	264
Daiquiri	4 oz	139
Eggnog	4 oz	370
Gin & Tonic	10 oz	212
Gin Rickey	4 oz	150
Mai Tai	4 oz	258
Manhattan	4 oz	187
Margarita	4 oz	254
Martini	4 oz	250
Old Fashioned	4 oz	179
Planters Punch	4 oz	200
Screwdriver	8 oz	232
Tom Collins (without mix)	10 oz	173
Tom Collins (with mix)	10 oz	252
LIQUEURS		
Anisette Cordial	2/3 oz	74
Benedictine	2/3 oz	69
Creme de Menthe	2/3 oz	67
Curacao	2/3 oz	54
General (fruit, chocolate, coffee)	2/3 oz	70-115
COCKTAIL MIXES		
Club Soda	8 oz	0
Cola	8 oz	96
Ginger Ale	8 oz	72
Mineral Water	8 oz	0
Quinine Water (Tonic)	8 oz	72
Seltzer	8 oz	0

DAY ONE

Breakfast at a Roadside Diner

1/2 sliced Banana
1 cup Cold or Hot Cereal
1 cup Low-Fat Milk
Coffee

Calories: 272
% Calories from Fat: 13
Mg. Sodium: 342

Lunch at Wendy's Fast Food

1 Baked Potato with Chili and Cheese
Diet Soda

Calories: 481
% Calories from Fat: 35
Mg. Sodium: 701

Dinner a la French Cuisine

Tossed Salad (2 cups) with Vinaigrette Dressing on the side
3 oz. Filet Mignon
Steamed New Red Potatoes (about 4 small potatoes)
Stir-fried Vegetable Medley (3/4 cup)
Fresh Strawberries with Chambord (1/2 cup)
Water
Coffee

Calories: 858
% Calories from Fat: 22
Mg. Sodium: 790

DAY TWO

Breakfast from Room Service

1/2 Grapefruit
Oat Bran Muffin
Coffee

Calories: 393
% Calories from Fat: 30
Mg. Sodium: 550

Lunch at the Salad Bar

Salad of Lettuce, Tomato, Red Onion, Alfalfa Sprouts (about 2 cups total)
1/4 cup Pickled Beets
1/4 cup Chick Peas
1/4 cup Tuna Salad
2 Tbsp. Low-Calorie Italian Dressing
8 oz. Skim Milk

Calories: 593
% Calories from Fat: 22
Mg. Sodium: 857

Dinner Italian Style

Steamed Clams (about 10 clams)
Linguini with Gorgonzola (about 1 1/2 cups)
Chicken in Wine Sauce (ask for about a 4-ounce portion)
Italian Ice (1 cup)
Coffee

Calories: 272
% Calories from Fat: 13
Mg. Sodium: 342

DAY THREE

Breakfast from a Deli

6 oz. Orange Juice
1 Egg, poached
Bagel, with cream cheese on the side
1/2 cup home fried Potatoes
Coffee, black

Calories: 541
% Calories from Fat: 37
Mg. Sodium: 560

Lunch at a Sandwich Shop

Grilled Chicken Breast (about 3 ounces)
with Lettuce, Tomato and Mustard
in a Pita Pocket Bread (3/4 of a bread)
3/4 cup Fresh Fruit
8 oz. Skim Milk

Calories: 589
% Calories from Fat: 16
Mg. Sodium: 1437

Dinner in a Seafood Restaurant

New England Clam Bake of:
Fish Chowder (1/2 cup)
Steamed Clams (about 10 to 15) with
drawn butter and lemon and clam broth (2 tsp.)
Boiled Maine Lobster (1 1/4 lb.) with
drawn butter and lemon sauce (2 tsp.)
Corn on the Cob (2 ears)
Coleslaw (1 cup)
Watermelon (2 cups)

Calories: 850
% Calories from Fat: 31
Mg. Sodium: 1350

DAY FOUR

Breakfast from Room Service

1/4 Cantaloupe Melon
English Muffin with 1 tsp. margarine
and 1 tsp. jelly
Coffee, black

Calories: 393
% Calories from Fat: 30
Mg. Sodium: 550

Lunch at McDonald's

Quarter-Pounder Hamburger
Small order Fries
Tossed Salad
with Reduced-Calorie Italian Dressing
8 oz. Skim Milk

Calories: 837
% Calories from Fat: 45
Mg. Sodium: 1373

*Chinese Dinner**

1 cup Hot and Sour Soup
1 1/2 cups Yu Hsiang Chicken
1 cup Shrimp with Broccoli and Mushrooms
2/3 cup Steamed White Rice
1 Fortune Cookie (Read fortune, discard cookie)
Hot Tea

Calories: 570
% Calories from Fat: 35
Mg. Sodium: 1300

**Be sure to request that soy sauce and MSG are not used.*

Five-Day Dine-Around Plan

DAY FIVE

Breakfast in the Hotel Coffee Shop

Fruit Cup
Whole Wheat Toast (2 slices) with
1 tsp. Margarine and 1 tsp. Jelly
1/2 cup Fruit Yogurt
Coffee

Calories: 495
% Calories from Fat: 16
Mg. Sodium: 366

Lunch at the Deli

1/2 Smoked Turkey Sandwich with Lettuce,
Tomato, Onion, and Mustard
on Pumpernickel Bread
1 Dill Pickle (if you can handle the sodium)
3/4 cup Cole Slaw
12 oz. Diet Soda

Calories: 464
% Calories from Fat: 28
Mg. Sodium: 1712 (with the pickle)
or 998 (without the pickle)

Mexican Dinner

2 cups Dinner Salad with Salsa as dressing
2 Chicken and Shrimp Fajitas
2/3 cup Mexican Rice
Water

Calories: 570
% Calories from Fat: 25
Mg. Sodium: 1100

Staying In Balance

Food choices are not the only thing you need to manage when you are on the road. Keeping your total self in balance—or maintaining homeostasis, as they say among the professionals—is your main challenge.

If you do your best to eat right, then work 46 hours without any rest, you're not staying in balance. Likewise, if you get plenty of rest, play two sets of tennis in the morning, but you don't eat breakfast or lunch, you're not doing your body a favor.

Staying in balance means just that: healthful eating, healthy exercise, at least 15 minutes daily of personal quiet time to manage the extra stress load imposed by travel, and taking care of any health problems that come up before they worsen into something serious.

The root meaning of *health* is wholeness. We need to strive for balance in all aspects of ourselves and our lives—acknowledging and addressing the needs of our bodies, minds, and spirits. Healthy people tend to feel good about themselves. They feel in control of their lives; they are committed to the work they do, and they are supportive and supported by the people around them.

Dr. William C. Menninger, founder of the world-famous Menninger Clinic in Topeka, Kansas, advises that for the best mental health and for the greatest emotional maturity, each individual should have a cause—a mission or an aim in life that is so constructive and so big that he or she has to keep working on it.

This doesn't mean that your job or vocation is necessarily your mission, but you'll want to take good care of yourself so that whatever you perceive your cause to be, you'll be healthy enough with sufficient energy to pursue it.

Psychologists say that it is not so much *what* happens in our lives, but how we handle what happens that counts. Attitude does indeed seem to be everything, particularly for those who travel in their work. Open-

Giant Travel Plaza on I-40 near Gallup, NM, is considered the best truck stop restaurant in the country. It features pies baked on the premises by three full-time bakers; made-from-scratch hamburgers; skin-on mashed potatoes; and hand-cut meats for Stroganoff and stews.

—Restaurant Hospitality

"The Swiss top the world in chocolate consumption with an average of 10.6 pounds per person a year. The U.S. came in 9th, averaging 4.7 pounds per person."

—International Cocoa Organization

minded, hopeful attitudes seem to help conquer adversity. Rigid, negative, inflexible attitudes, on the other hand, prevent people from enjoying even the good times in their lives, as well as decrease their ability to cope with stress.

Our best advice for the business traveler for staying in balance:

1. Always expect the unexpected.

2. Have a sense of humor about whatever you find in your travels.

3. "Go with the flow." Remember that swimming upstream wastes your energy. If something really bothers you, you'll want to react, but choose only the most important issues. There's a lot of hassle in a life of travel, and bending with the winds usually is better for your health.

4. Finally, be prepared. Try to plan ahead for the contingencies.

2

EXERCISE ON THE ROAD

Exercise is "big" in America. Yet many of us are quick to use business travel as an excuse to avoid anything that resembles "working out."

That whole working-out idea is a turn-off. What we need to do is recondition ourselves to think of exercise as play—something most of us did quite well when we were younger.

Most of us find it difficult to play. We believe work is good. It reflects well on our character. Play, on the other hand, is frivolous.

True, many adults "play" sports, but watch them and you'll see they are merely shifting their competitive drive from the job to the playing field. The primary goal is no longer to have fun but to win.

So, as you travel, give yourself time to lighten up. Work is good, but life is just too short to continually strive for money, fame, success—or whatever—without enjoyment.

Note How You Feel

The goal of exercise (maybe movement is a better way to think of it) is to help you feel good. If the sensations don't feel good, it's okay to change them. The old adage "no pain, no gain" is hogwash!

Instead of setting a distant goal such as increasing muscle size or lowering heart rate, just concentrate on pleasant feelings. Ironically, this fun approach to exercise results in more rapid benefits. This should not be surprising since there is less emotional stress when you are having fun. Unfortunately, according to a recent survey, only about 10% of Americans exercise because they enjoy it.

The most popular exercise is walking, with over 67 million participants, followed by swimming (63 million) and bicycling (54 million).

—National Sporting Goods Association

Pound for pound, the strongest muscle in your body is the masseter—the muscle that closes the jaws.

In *You Don't Have to Go Home from Work Exhausted,* psychologist Ann McGee Cooper says the subconscious doesn't know the difference between real or imagined fun. In other words, looking forward to having fun can give you the same energy boost as actually having fun.

Conversely, viewing a forthcoming workout as drudgery begins to drain you even before you start exercising.

If you can learn to relax and enjoy exercising and to begin appreciating your kinesthetic sensations, you will find the time to exercise. You will not make excuses to avoid exercising. Attitude is everything.

Environment

Today's business trips often involve changes in weather conditions. Keep these changes in mind as you plan your "play."

A warm climate may feel delightful but it's the most dangerous for exercise. It may be difficult to lose body heat fast enough and before you know it you're suffering from a heat illness—heat cramps, heat exhaustion, dehydration, or heat stroke.

Plan to reduce your pace when you exercise in a warm climate. When it's hot, your heart has to pump extra blood to the skin to cool your body. The problem is even more complicated when it's humid. In that situation, the sweat evaporates very slowly so the blood is cooled very slowly.

During hot spells, the weather bureau will broadcast the heat index (a combination of temperature and humidity). If it's high enough, a warning will be issued.

Don't wait for the warning. Keep in touch with your body. If you are starting to sweat more than usual, slow down or stop.

Drink water before, during, and after exercise. If you begin to get a headache, a little dizzy, and have a weak rapid pulse, find a cool spot, drink a lot of water, and lie down.

As a preventive measure, walk in the shade when it's

hot. Ultraviolet rays are harmful to your skin, so always use sunblock with a sun protection factor (SPF) of at least 15.

Exercising in the cold at moderate to intense levels is not as dangerous as exercising in the heat. Surprisingly, most problems arise because people tend to dress too warmly.

The idea is to dress in layers to keep moisture away from the skin. The first layer should consist of materials such as cotton, marine wool, or polypropylene. Over that wear windbreaker material such as Gortex, PTFE-Film, or Versatech. That combination will suffice for most cold, wet days.

If the temperature and wind combine to have a very cold effect, add a middle layer of a heavier material like wool.

If you are going to be only mildly active, as in strolling, you will have to dress more warmly. For short exposures, take special care to heavily insulate the hands and feet.

For longer periods of exposure, though, it is more important to keep your torso well insulated to help maintain your core body temperature. A down-filled vest is excellent.

Always be aware of the wind chill factor when preparing to venture into the elements on cold days. And most importantly seek and follow the advice of knowledgeable local residents.

Since cold air tends to be dry, don't be surprised if you experience a temporary hacking cough after strenuous exercise in the cold. Also, watch out for patches of ice. Southerners quickly learn, usually the hard way, why the phrase "as slick as ice" was conceived.

Altitude

Altitude can cause some problems if you decide to get out and exercise. Denver (the mile high city) and Mexico City at 7,575 feet can literally take your breath away. Even at 3,000 feet you lose 5% of your aerobic capacity. And the higher you go, the harder it is for the heart to deliver

Sitting for a long time? Tap your toes for several minutes while keeping your heels on the floor. This pushes blood up your legs and reduces swelling of the legs.

"I won't say I'm out of condition now—but I even puff going downstairs."
Dick Gregory

oxygen to your muscles. Therefore, at high altitudes, say, over 5,000 feet, you may want to take it easy during exercise.

Pollution

Air pollution also complicates exercising. When the pollution index is high, exercise indoors. Air conditioner filters help to clean the air. If a city has a pollution problem, its newspaper will print the pollution index each day.

Pollution levels are generally highest during the peak commuting hours (6 to 9 a.m. — 4 to 7 p.m.) Plan accordingly, especially if you have a pulmonary disorder such as asthma, chronic bronchitis, or emphysema.

When and How Long?

As a general rule, you should exercise three times a week. Once a week will not improve fitness—and injuries are likely to occur. More than four sessions a week also tends to increase chance for injury.

The duration of each exercise session should be at least 20 or preferably 30 minutes. At that level you will acquire most of the health benefits of exercise. If you want to exercise for 60 minutes because you enjoy doing so, fine. You won't gain much more in health but you will gain more in physical fitness.

Remember, you don't have to exercise for 30 minutes straight. A recent review of scientific studies by the Centers for Disease Control and Prevention revealed that adequate health benefits can also be achieved by exercising in small increments throughout the day for a total of 30 minutes at least three days per week.

If you are on a typical three-day-a-week exercise schedule and a five-day business jaunt is looming, exercise the day before you depart. That means you only have to be concerned with two exercise sessions during your trip. Before you have even reached your destination your exercise commitment is one-third met.

If you have long work days, as people often do on business trips, consider short, easy sessions at the end of each day. They have the additional advantage of being very relaxing. With mild sessions you may not be improving your health and fitness, but you'll be maintaining what you have. And that's what many people on the road are happy to accomplish.

If you are too exhausted for even mild exercise sessions, use stairs instead of elevators throughout the day and walk at least part of the way between your hotel room and the meeting location instead of taking a taxi the entire way. These short exercise breaks serve to reduce fatigue and do give you some exercise benefit. Anything is better than nothing.

The fatigue of meetings is not caused by physical exhaustion but by mental and emotional stress. Exercise often perks you up.

Exercise in the Car

When you're stuck in a traffic jam or waiting for a long train to move through an intersection, try some simple exercises to help you relax. You might be surprised at how fast the time goes when you have something to work on.

One simple exercise is sometimes called the "I must" push. The exercise works equally well for both genders in strengthening the pectoral muscles.

Begin the "I musts" by putting your hands together in a praying position, with your wrists in front of your forehead. Press your hands together as hard as you want, keeping in mind that the harder you press the greater the strength building stimulus. Do not hold a strong contraction for over a second or two.

You can do ten repetitions with your hands in the same place or you can move them up and down in front of the chest and head while rhythmically performing the one-second contractions. Another variation is to move the hands from side to side, diagonally, in a circular fashion, or in a combination of them all.

Another simple exercise begins with the elbows at your waist. The elbows can be

"Some 35 to 60 percent of the average manager's day is taken up by meetings . . . . What can you do to make meetings more efficient? Avoid comfortable chairs, coffee, and pastries."

—Working Woman

"Chances, during our lifetime, that the Earth will be struck by an object from space large enough to possibly end civilization: 1 in 10,000."

—Men's Health magazine

extended or bent. Then press your arms forcefully against your sides. These side squeezers can be done anywhere, including in meetings.

Another variation is to put your elbows against the back of your chair, or wall, and push. Make sure the chair is a strong one; chairs have been known to explode when the force is unusually strong (or chairs unusually weak).

Still another variation is to put both palms directly over your navel and push. Of course, when you do these exercises during meeting breaks, some people may stare. Just explain that the exercises keep your mind clear and sharp so you can think better.

The muscles of the neck are often neglected but they must not be overlooked. An excellent exercise is to exaggerate a shoulder shrug. Bring your shoulders forward, raise them as high as you can, and then push them back and down. As with all muscles, after you finish they will be very relaxed — unless you exercise them too strenuously. Shoulder shrugs are great for reducing the tension built up during a busy day.

For front and side neck muscles, place your palms (fingers pointing upward) on your forehead and apply resistance as you slowly flex your head forward. Do only three repetitions if you haven't exercised the neck before and don't exert much force.

Next, lock your fingers and place your palms on the back of your head and apply resistance; don't extend your head to the rear. Then, place your right palm against your head above the ear and flex your head to the right, against resistance. Do the same thing to the left.

If you are prone to headaches, you may find it more effective to not apply resistance to the head movements. Just lower your head forward slowly and let it "hang" for 10 to 20 seconds. Then raise it to the normal position. Repeat three times.

Do the same thing to the left and then to the right. As the days go by, increase the number of repetitions to ten.

In a Plane

Seat exercises are becoming quite fashionable on overseas flights. After all, no one wants to sit still for 8 or 9 hours. Some airlines offer in-flight videos, which are quite entertaining as weil as healthful. British Airways offers the following suggestions for keeping fit while you sit.

HANDS: With your palm to the ground, stretch the thumb toward the wrist as you breathe out. Repeat with the other hand.

- With the palm up, stretch each finger down as you breathe out.
- Rotate your wrists five to ten times clockwise and then counterclockwise.
- Shake your hands out.

NECK: Rotate your neck slowly five times in each direction.

- Raise your shoulders towards your ears, breathe out, drop, and repeat four or five times.
- Rotate your shoulders backwards five times and forwards five times.
- Turn to face the back of your seat, keeping your hips square. Repeat three to five times.

HEAD: With fingertips, lightly tap the top and sides of your head.

- With finger tips, gently massage from temples to jaw.
- Rest your head forward on your thumbs, then squeeze along eyebrows with the thumb and forefinger.
- Massage from under eyes along cheekbones, then from either side of nostrils down upper jaw.

To remain as comfortable as possible in flight, do not cross your legs for prolonged periods or keep the back of your legs against the front of the seat. And every hour, walk about the cabin or spend a few minutes 'walking in place.'

—Traveling Healthy

"The average American spends 49 hours seeing doctors...and 64 hours waiting to see doctors."

—In An Average Lifetime

- Massage along lower jaw.

- Rotate jaw, circling five times, left then right.

ANKLES: Rotate your ankles ten times clockwise and ten times counterclockwise.

- Spread your toes and point your foot toward you, then clench and point your foot away. Alternate five times.

- With your feet on the floor, raise your heels, then relax. Repeat 20 or 30 times.

If you have extra time in an airport, try to do some stretches and take a walk.

When You Get There

More than 200 years ago Thomas Jefferson, recommended, "Habituate yourself to walking fast without fatigue." That is still excellent advice. And you don't need special garb. Can you imagine the noble Tom in spandex britches?

With a little imagination you can create hundreds of subtle and not so subtle variations to make the activity more interesting.

For information on race walking (striding) write to the Walkers Club of America, 445 E. 86th St., New York, NY 10128. Include a stamped, self-addressed envelope.

Walking is a more flexible activity than jogging in terms of where you can do it. If you walk briskly, 20 to 30 minutes is sufficient to achieve aerobic benefits. Since crowds may force you to walk fairly slowly, however, you'll have to walk for a longer period to get the same aerobic effect.

Wear athletic shoes, preferably the walking type, whenever you can. Make sure they are broken in; you don't want to be limping unnecessarily when you arrive at your destination.

Anytime you are in an unfamiliar city and plan to walk or jog, get advice from the hotel staff. Ask more than one person about the safest route. And use common sense. With awareness you can usually sense when you're in a neighborhood that welcomes you for the wrong reasons.

If you don't feel safe in the neighborhood, try walking in place in your room. This is a must if the air pollution is severe enough to produce such symptoms as tightening in the chest, eye irritation, dryness of the throat, headache, and difficulty breathing.

Most exercise videos demonstrate how to walk in place to get the most out of it. If you haven't seen one, vigorously pump your arms forward and back while lifting your knees high. Lean forward a bit at the waist. It's very good exercise and you can create a lot of variety by changing the tempo and how high you lift your knees. You can also move forwards, backwards, to the sides, or turn in a circle.

Anytime you walk, jog, or engage in an activity that involves running (such as tennis) for a prolonged time, you should stretch the calf muscles before and after the event. That reduces soreness and the chances for injury.

No Machines Needed

A number of simple exercises can take the place of a session with machines. Do every exercise slowly and over as long a range of motion as you can. That will develop the muscles over the entire range of motion and will also stretch the muscles you are contracting, which is highly desirable. The slow pace allows you to move gracefully. More importantly, good joint mobility helps reduce aches and pains in the joints areas. This effect is magnified as you get older.

Relax briefly after each repetition to allow blood to move through the muscles you're "working." Do ten repetitions for each exercise and, of course, exercise both sides of the body.

Concentrate on the feelings with every repetition. You'll probably enjoy the sensations immediately or after a few sessions. If not, vary the exercises so you do enjoy them. Generally this can be achieved merely by making an exercise a bit

The airline with the most room between seats is TWA, which recently increased the space between rows from 31 to 36 inches.

—Men's Health magazine

Skeletal muscles account for about 40 percent of your body weight. These are the muscles that allow you to move and do physical activity.

easier or by varying your repetitions.

Leg exercises tend to warm up the body and are a good place to start.

Lunges are excellent for the muscles at the front the thighs. Place your hands on your hips and while keeping your upper body erect, step forward with one foot. The first step need only be a few inches forward of the stationary foot. The rear foot remains in place and you can allow the leg to bend or remain straight. Each step should be further than the previous one. The last step, say, the tenth one, will find you in a deep lunge position. Then return to the starting position.

Lunges are a very strenuous activity. You can make them easier without feeling guilty. You are the best judge of what you can or should do. Stop when you want before you reach the deep lunge position.

You can do lunges to the rear by keeping one foot in place and stepping backwards. Similarly, you can do side lunges by stepping with one foot to the side. For variety, the direction of the lunges can be mixed. They can be done in alternate fashion or in groups of ten, or whatever. A little creativity will make the exercises more enjoyable.

Knee bends (pliés, if you are a dancer) are also excellent. Hold onto the dresser for balance if you wish. Don't squat too low or you will excessively stretch the ligaments of the knee joint and thus weaken it. Don't go any lower than a 90° angle at the knees.

A chair behind you makes a reliable and safe reference point. Also, do not poke your buttocks rearward when you are going down. That takes the stress off your quadriceps—exactly where you want it.

It is important to keep the hips tucked a bit under you through the entire exercise. There would be a lot less lower back pain if people would learn to walk this way—not to the point of looking ridiculous but enough to reduce the curvature of the lower back. If a 90° squat is too difficult or you just don't feel like going that low, you don't have to.

It makes no difference whether you point your feet directly forward or at an angle to the side, a lá ballet, as long as you keep your knees over your feet instead of pointing inward, which most people tend to do. By keeping the knees over your feet you will strengthen your arches.

The simple exercise of rising up on the balls of your feet will strengthen your calves. You'll find it easier to balance if you hold onto a door frame or dresser while doing these.

For a better stretch between contractions merely lean over from the waist with your forearms resting on the dresser. To exercise at different angles begin the exercise with your toes pointing a bit inward. With each repetition point your toes a little more to the sides.

You can exercise your hamstring muscles (at the back of the thighs) while standing erect and lifting your foot. This will naturally cause your knee to bend. But don't let the knee move forward—keep it next to the other knee or let it move backward a little. Do it slowly and lift it high. You'll feel it. Don't try to bring your foot back as far as you can. That will result in a temporary "swayback."

Directly above the hamstrings are the gluteal muscles. These extend the legs to the rear. The lunges and knee bends described earlier involve the gluteals. Walking up stairs is also an excellent exercise. Walk slowly and enjoy the sensations. Better yet, take two stairs at a time.

In Bed

If you're lying in bed watching T.V. and the program is not capturing your attention, roll over onto your back. Then draw your heels close to your buttocks. From this position lift your hips toward the ceiling. Your quadriceps also get a workout.

For a different type of gluteal exercise lie on your stomach and lift your leg rearward toward the ceiling. Keep the legs straight. This exercise is called a hip extension.

If you have lower back problems, it would be bet-

"A body of water keeps your body in shape on the road, says Walking Magazine. Walking in water—pool or beach, for example, thigh deep or deeper gives an aerobic workout without the pounding of most sports."

—Traveling Healthy

"Those who do not find time to exercise will have to find time for illness."
Old Proverb

ter to stand erect for hip extensions. Do not swing the leg like a pendulum. Good form for this exercise is to keep the hips tucked under as in the "bump and grind" performed by artistic dancers. These maneuvers exercise the muscles of the midsection rather well. And you'll probably enjoy the sensations associated with it. If you are a football fan, you'll sometimes be treated to a demonstration of this exotic exercise by a player celebrating a touchdown.

At Meetings

You may want to exercise your gluteals and quadriceps simultaneously while sitting in a vehicle or meeting. If so, simply position your feet so the lower legs are roughly perpendicular to the floor. Then slowly push down while consciously squeezing your buttocks together.

Bumps and grinds (or you can use the more technical term "combined posterior and lateral hip rotations") also serve to strengthen the abdominal muscles and loosen the muscles of the lower back.

A more traditional abdominal exercise is the sit-up. Traditional doesn't always mean appropriate, however. Indeed, if done incorrectly, sit-ups can be one of the most harmful exercises, especially if you have lower back problems.

Sit-ups create the highly prized washboard effect (if you are lean). The muscles at the sides of your body (the obliques) also contract strongly to help you do curl-ups.

Trunk twisters are a good exercise to do during meeting breaks. The most common way to do a trunk twister is to stand with your feet about shoulder width apart and rotate your trunk. Keep your knees locked, though. That prevents the hips from rotating. If the hips rotate, the purpose of the exercise is completely defeated. You want your hips to be stationary while your trunk (upper body) rotates.

If you have trouble keeping the hips stationary while standing, rotate your trunk while sitting on a firm surface such as a dresser or a chair without arms. Your hips will not rotate — guaranteed. Perform trunk twisters slowly and don't rotate too far. You may very well end up with an injury—usually to the back.

Stomach muscles are sometimes forgotten in exercise plans but deserve a good workout daily. All you have to do is slowly suck in the stomach for about ten repetitions. Do these "suck-ins" two or three times a day. You can do them in a car, at your desk, during a meeting, or anytime.

The most important abdominal exercise is good posture. With proper posture, the abdominal muscles are always partially contracting, even though you're not aware of it.

Essentially, good posture means standing erect in a relaxed fashion—the head is not thrust forward, there is no slumping of the shoulders, the "stomach" does not protrude, and the hips do not tilt forward to create a swayback.

Strong abdominal muscles are a must for everyone. They are the basis for good posture. They allow you to move more efficiently, greatly reduce the chances for lower back pain, and result in a more pleasing appearance. Strong abdominal muscles resist the pull of gravity against the internal organs thus keeping them in place.

For the upper body, the most important exercise is the push-up. It is one of the very best for strengthening the chest (pectoral) muscles. At the same time it also exercises the shoulder muscles (deltoids) and the muscles on the back of the arm (triceps).

If you want to "work" primarily the pectoral muscles with push-ups, the exercises should be done with the elbows out to the side.

If you want to exercise mainly the triceps, do the push-ups with your elbows close to the sides of your body. Try them both ways and you'll quickly feel the difference.

Good form for a traditional push-up involves keeping your feet together with your legs extended. Your hands will be at the level of your chest with fingers pointing forward.

At meetings run by Willow Shire, a vice president at Digital Equipment, you'd better be on time—if not, she'll fine you $1. She turns the money over to St. Jude Children's Research Hospital in Memphis.

—Working Woman

Some frequent flyers who carry their baggage suffer from neck and shoulder pain. The problem stems from luggage pulling on ligaments. Discomfort disappears with the application of heat and, in some cases, physical therapy—and by using luggage carts or checking luggage.

—Traveling Healthy

Start with your chest on the floor. Take a deep breath and push so as to straighten your arms. As you go up, slowly exhale. Do not hold your breath. In fact, never hold your breath during the most difficult phase of any repetition. Inhale during the easy phase. When you come back to the floor your chest should touch —not your abdomen.

If this strict push-up is too difficult, have your knees touch the floor instead of your toes. You can also begin with several of the strict push-ups and follow-up with a number of the easier ones.

Another way to make push-ups easier is to do them from a standing position with your hands on the edge of a dresser instead of on the floor. You can lean as little or as much as you want to make them as easy or hard as you want.

The easier variations of push-ups, or any exercise, are as good for a person who is not very strong as the strict version is for a strong person.

Use the Parks

Most cities have parks with walking or jogging paths. Some even have a "Vita Course." That's basically a jogging course (but there's nothing to stop you from walking) with a station every 50 or so yards that directs you to do a number of push-ups or sit-ups, etc.

Some cities have trails based upon the Swedish "Fartlek" design that requires walking or running at slow and fast speeds on level and hilly ground.

If there are no trails, try a walking tour of the city. While a 30-minute walk on a treadmill can seem interminably boring, a 60-minute jaunt through the heart of the city will not be—provided, of course, the situation is safe.

Free Time

Just as exercise should be enjoyable, so should your business sojourn — and ideally, your meetings. Unfortunately, most people seem to take themselves so seriously they end up not having any fun.

If you're cooped up all day and into the evening, the people who planned the meetings have been remiss. They would be wise to schedule at least one 15-minute walking break in the morning and one in the afternoon. It would also drastically reduce the negative emotions that often arise in meetings.

You don't have to limit walking to formal exercise sessions. You may want to walk between your hotel and meeting rooms. If they are in the same building, take the stairs instead of taking the elevator. Those mini-sessions add up.

A word of caution, for security reasons the doors at each floor will sometimes open only from the corridor side. Nobody wants to walk up 24 flights of stairs only to find a locked door.

According a 1992 survey by the National Sporting Goods Association (NSGA), walking was found to be the most popular participant activity (67.8 million). Swimming was number two at 63.1 million participants. Aerobic "dancing" snared another 27.8 million.

Swimming

Fortunately, many hotels have swimming pools. Swimming is wonderful if you've been traveling or sitting in meetings. It relaxes muscles and is gentle on the joints.

If you are not a good swimmer, try a jogging vest. The flotation device allows you to jog while in the water and is excellent for taking the travel kinks out of your body. Take advantage of a pool if one is available.

Biking

Bicycle riding is number three on the NSGA's popularity list, with 54.6 million enthusiasts. In some cities, particularly in resort areas, you can rent a bicycle.

If time permits, take advantage of that for sightseeing. It is not a great fitness enhancer, because traffic conditions often prevent you from going fast enough, but it's better than nothing. Besides, it can be very relaxing and that, next to fun, is the main reason for exercising.

Looking for a place to swim? The American Lap Swimmers Association Swimmers' Guide provides updated information on 1,200 pools, including admission prices and hours of operation. To purchase the book, call (800) 431-9111.

Prepare for Takeoff—

"The highest recorded decibel level of a snoring sleeper is 90. A jet airplane at takeoff is 100."

—Men's Health magazine

When you rent a bicycle be sure to get a map and some advice from the proprietor on where to go.

Weight Training

Weight training is now considered an important part of a total fitness program. Aerobic exercises do result in some increase in strength, but weight training is more efficient and specific.

Of course, no one needs huge body parts unless he is a competing bodybuilder, football player, or professional wrestler. In fact, massive muscles put an unnecessary burden on the heart just to carry the muscles around. It is helpful, though, to be strong enough to make chores easier and to look "toned." And this is true for men and women.

If your trip is for five days or less, race walking (forcefully using the arms and a pronounced hip action) will certainly maintain your total body strength. So will swimming. Even brisk walking in a normal manner will do so. And if you've been weight training intensely for only a few months, a one-week recovery is a sound idea.

Heavy resistance training doesn't build muscle tissue and strength. Such training merely increases the tension in muscles—and that tension provides the stimulus for muscle growth. Actual growth occurs only with a subsequent period of relaxation with a proper diet.

If you're using a business trip as a recovery period, it's best not to eliminate all activity. You can walk, swim, or ride a bike in moderation.

Since weight training with machines is high on NSGA's list of sports participation (39.4 million), it is reasonable to assume many business people are involved in the activity and continue their programs while on the road. Anyone not engaged in such a program should not begin while traveling. It will be a waste of time unless the equipment is identical to what you will use at home.

You are better off not using machines if they are different than the ones you are used to. You'll only be using them for a few days so any improvement will be minor. But even a mild injury (such as intense soreness) is going to knock you out of action for a week or more. You're taking a chance of backsliding with virtually nothing to gain.

If there is no gym in your hotel and you feel you must adhere to a strength-building program, try exercising in your room. For every machine exercise there are many exercises you can do to stimulate the same muscles—without using machines. An example is the bench press which strongly involves the chest muscles. Push-ups have the same effect.

In the ideal business traveler's world, hotels would have stationary bikes or cross-country ski machines available through room service. Although that might seem unrealistic, if enough people asked for the service, some hotels might respond.

"The decline of leisure is more than just a fashionable catchphrase; it's a fact. According to a Harvard University study, the average person had 19.8 days off in 1981. In 1991 the figure dropped to 16.1—a decline of almost 20 percent."

—Travel Holiday

3

RELIEVING YOUR STRESS

There are bound to be extra stressors on the road. We've already mentioned quite a few. So, here are some tips for how to manage your total stress load, not just when you are traveling, but anytime.

Self-Talk

Have you ever watched children tying their shoes? If they are just learning, they are usually talking to themselves. Without this chatter, tying a shoe is difficult.

Research suggests that this "self-talk" is also useful to adults, especially when they switch from negative to positive talk. In fact, do you realize who you talk to the most every day? Yourself! If you start paying attention, you'll probably be surprised at how many negative messages you're giving yourself. Are you saying, "I shouldn't have done this or that?" Or "I shouldn't have to put up with this." Or "This flight is awful. At this rate, I'll never make it to my meeting on time."

Negative thoughts create tension. Make a conscious choice to be encouraging to yourself rather than discouraging. Whenever you find yourself saying, "I can't...," or "I won't...," or "I shouldn't...," remind yourself of that childhood tale: *The Little Engine That Could.* All the Little Engine did was say, "I think I can. I think I can. I think I can." And he did!

You may want to use the examples on the next page to work out some self-talk possibilities for yourself.

Johnson, J.L., R.N., Ph.D., and Klein, L. I Can Cope. CHRONIMED Publishing. Minneapolis: 1994.

"Complete freedom from stress is death."
Dr. Hans Selye

Travelers' top causes of headaches include traffic, lack of leg room, and fast food.

- It might be difficult, but I am going to go through the argument with them again.

- I must turn down that extra work. I can cope now, but with extra I will be overloaded.

- I know I'm being yelled at, but she is under stress, too, and has probably had a very bad day.

Meditation

Many people find that meditation is helpful for relieving stress. Whereas with self-talk you give yourself up-to-the-minute positive suggestions, with meditation you attempt to relax, putting your body at rest, and when you are completely calm, you listen to whatever messages your body might have for you.

There are a number of forms of meditation. One of the easiest to learn and to practice is called "Progressive Muscle Relaxation."

The point of this exercise is to become keenly aware of the differences between relaxed and tense muscle groups. Accordingly, you progress through all the major muscle groups, alternately flexing and relaxing muscles until you have covered all the muscles in the body and have achieved a state of calm.

Before you begin:

- Choose a quiet, comfortable place.
- Loosen any tight clothing and take off your shoes.
- Sit or lie as comfortably as possible.
- Close your eyes, uncross your legs, and rest your hands flat, with your palms turned upward.

Then relax each part of the body.

Tense each part of the body as described on the next page for a count of 10. Take a deep breath in, feel the tension, then let the tension go as you breathe out. Use self-talk by quietly saying the word "relax" as you do so.

TOES: Curl your toes toward you or down to the floor.

CALVES: Point your toes toward your face.

BUTTOCKS: Push your buttocks hard against your chair or bed, at the same time trying to make your body feel as heavy as possible.

ABDOMEN: Tense your abdomen, as if preparing to receive a punch in the stomach.

SHOULDERS*:* Shrug your shoulders as high as they can possibly go.

THROAT: Use your chin to press your throat hard.

NECK AND HEAD: Press your neck and head against the backs of your shoulders, stretching your neck as you do so.

FACE: Tighten as many facial muscles as possible, including forehead, jaw, chin, and nose.

The Short Form

When you don't have 15 or 20 minutes to complete the total relaxation procedure described above, use the following actions, tensing and relaxing as above. You can practice this abbreviated version anywhere: on an airplane, in a meeting, in a bathroom, or anyplace.

1. Tighten and tense the whole upper part of your body.

2. Pull in your abdomen or tense your buttocks.

3. Try to force your body off the chair by pressing the soles of your feet hard against the floor and trying to lift your body using your calf and other leg muscles.

Two industries with the highest rates of job stress: telecommunications and financial services.

—Psychology Today

Airports that provoke the most headaches...

1. Chicago O'Hare
2. Atlanta's William Hartsfield
3. New York's JFK;
4. Los Angeles International
5. New York's La Guardia.

—Excedrin Travel Headache Report

The key to relaxation in both instances is to note the difference between stressed muscles and relaxed muscles. Work toward achieving a relaxed posture more frequently, and use meditation any time you need it to relieve stress.

Guided Imagery

Guided imagery is a wonderful relaxation technique that uses both self-talk and muscle relaxation, and it brings the other senses into play as well. Dr. Joseph Juliano, an endocrinologist and author of *When Diabetes Complicates Your Life,* recommends that you have a friend with a voice you like make a tape for you of your favorite guided imagery. Of course, to use the tape you should have a Walkman™ with you. This is a good idea, not just for meditation, but for listening to relaxing music as well.

Here's a script of a favorite guided-imagery meditation. It comes from a book about relieving pain *(You Can Relieve Pain: How Guided Imagery Can Help You Reduce Pain or Eliminate It Altogether,* by Ken Dachman and John Lyons. HarperCollins, New York: 1990).

Imagine Yourself...

Imagine yourself lying back in a small boat. You have thick, soft cushions tucked under you and lying around you. You feel comfortable and safe. Your boat is floating down a narrow channel. The sun is filtering through the leaves in the tops of the oak trees that arch above you. You see the shadows of the leaves flickering on your body.

Underneath you, you feel the gentle rocking of the boat as you float along on the current. Water laps softly against the sides of your boat. It's early summer: so it's warm but not sticky or humid. You float downstream. Smell the forest smells and the smells of the waterway. Let all your sensors investigate the world around you.

Look over the side of the boat. See the fish swimming in the stream. Notice their color and their shapes as they dart back and forth under the water and under the boat. They look as if they're being reflected in a fun house mirror, distorted by the moving water. Let your hand trail in the stream. Feel the refreshing coolness of the water.

Splash some water on your face. Look around you at the banks of the stream. What do you see? Try to remember everything. Look up at the sky. Be aware of everything around you. Feel content and serene as you drift on.

You're coming to a tunnel now, but you've been through this tunnel before, so you know what to expect. Darkness, then escape. A good place for shade when it's hot. As you float into the tunnel, you can't see anything except the sunlight sparkling on the water at the other end. Your boat is drifting slowly into the darkness, and your mind wanders. Where does it go? It's always moving, into the past, back into the present, probing into the future. Linger into the tunnel; dream in the tunnel; stay as long as you want.

As you come out of the tunnel, feel yourself being covered by golden sunshine. The sunlight wraps itself around you and brings you energy and makes you smile. You glide out of the tunnel and come to a lake. You float on the lake. A cool breeze sweeps across your body. The lake is tranquil. It's nearly silent. Feel the quiet.

Be aware of everything: the gentle motion of the boat, the warmth of the sun, the fragrances (there's lavender growing somewhere along the lake). Be aware of the sounds of just drifting along. Let yourself feel these sensations.

You're floating on the lake. Your little boat is circling like a satellite, not going anywhere else. This lake is just where you want to be.

Spend as much time on the lake as you want. When you are ready to come back from this lake, come back slowly and gently. Remind yourself of where you are, open your eyes and look around you. You feel completely refreshed and alert.

Guided Imagery

Guided Imagery

There are many relaxation tapes available in book stores. One of our favorites comes from Valley of the Sun in Malibu, California. It is from *Stress Control: RX17,* and is a digital-holophonic audio cassette by Dick Sutphen. (You can order this by calling 1-800-225-4717.) Here's the script:

A Journey Into Deep Relaxation

Take a very deep breath and quiet your mind. I want you to imagine being on the sandy beach of a peaceful tropical island. Visualize the scenes I am describing to the very best of your ability, mentally creating every detail of these pictures in your mind. Make them real: perceive the sounds and the smells that accompany your impressions, and sense the feeling this environment generates within you.

It's almost sunrise... the sky is just dark enough for you to see the last few stars.... The palm trees that line this tropical beach are silhouetted against the sky. Experience the fresh salt sea air .... You are totally at peace here. All your mental and physical desires are satisfied, and you experience this environment in total peace.

So watch the stars, listen to the swish of the palm trees in the wind, totally experience this peaceful environment. And as you do, feel your physical body relaxing—beginning with both of your feet at the same time. Feel your feet relaxing—and the relaxing power moves up into your lower legs, relaxing all your muscles as it goes. And on up into your upper legs—permeating every cell and every atom.

And the sky is becoming lighter and lighter. All is silent but for the calls of the sea gulls and the lapping of the waves. The stars are slowly fading away. And as you observe this beautiful environment, you feel the relaxing power in the fingers of your hands, relaxing your hands. Feel your hands relaxing and feel the relaxing power move up into your forearms. And on up to your upper arms, just completely relaxing your fingers, your hands, your forearms, and your upper arms.

And you now become more aware of the sea gulls announcing the new day, as the darkness slowly fades away and the sky becomes lighter... bluer... bluer. And the horizon now begins to glow red, then yellow golden. The first rays of the sun touch the tops of the palm trees.

And now as the sun slowly rises, watch the light illuminating the palms as it moves down the trunk of the trees. And within, you feel a warmth in your spine, as the relaxing power flows through your spine and into your back muscles, relaxing your back. And it moves on up into your neck and shoulder muscles, which now become loose and limp... loose and limp... just completely relaxed.

And now the sun falls across your body, bathing you in a golden light. You shiver in response as you absorb the essence and energy. Feel the sun on your skin and perceive it filling your body to overflowing with energy; the relaxing power now moves on up the back of your neck and into your scalp, relaxing your scalp; it drains down into your facial muscles, relaxing all the muscles in your face.

Your jaw is relaxed. Allow a little space between your teeth. And your throat is relaxed. Your entire body is now relaxed all over in every way. Now notice how the sun reflects on the surface of the water: sparkling—sparkling yellow and gold. Flickering reflections of the sun that is now rising into the yellow golden sky sparkle on the water.

Enjoy this environment. You can swim or walk along the beach. Or simply lie back in the warm sand. And as you do, you'll begin to hear a sound that will relax you even more... even more... even more.

And you are now relaxed and at ease and in total control. At this relaxed level, your subconscious mind is open and receptive to positive suggestions:

You are relaxed and at ease... relaxed and at ease... relaxed and at ease. You detach from worldly pressures and retreat to a calm inner space. Every day in every way, you become more peaceful and harmonious. You accept other people just

Guided Imagery

as they are, without expectations. You handle your responsibilities with harmonious ease. Negativity flows through you without affecting you. You peacefully accept the things you cannot change and change the things you can. You are at peace with yourself, the world, and everyone in it.

This is a useful script to use at bedtime. Most models of the battery-operated Walkman shut themselves off, so you can listen to this script and then drift off to sleep on that sunny beach. Or you can end the exercise by coming awake slowly, reminding yourself where you are, and telling yourself how relaxed, refreshed, and alert you are. Keep a copy of a relaxation script among the papers in your briefcase or on your portable computer. Sometimes just reading it helps to remind you how to relax.

Body Scanning

This technique for relaxing sounds exotic, but it really isn't. It's simply a way to become more aware of your body.

Lie down on the floor and close your eyes. Starting with your toes, think your way up your body asking yourself, "Where do I feel tension?" If you discover your jaw muscles are tight, exaggerate them slightly by tightening them more. Remind yourself that this takes effort and if continued over a long period of time you will become exhausted. Then relax those muscles and move on to the next source of tension.

Try doing this just before you leave for work and again before you go to bed. It takes about five minutes and is a great pick-me-up.

Daily Coping Resources

In addition to the relaxation exercises listed above, there are numerous ways to make stress more manageable on a daily basis. Dr. Paul Terry and Dr. Allan Kind, in their book *It's Your Body*, suggest that you make a list of those stress reducers that work for you and keep it in your briefcase or on your laptop computer as a reminder that you are in charge of the stress in your life.

Laughter, Just For The Health of It

Dale Anderson, M.D., a physician at Park Nicollet Medical Clinic in Minneapolis and a nationally renowned speaker on the subject of humor and health, routinely prescribes humor to help his patients improve their overall sense of health and well-being.

"Laughter raises your 'inner uppers,'" says Anderson. "When you laugh, your body produces endorphins—the chemicals that have a sedative-like effect for people who are stressed.

"Next time you feel tense, look in the mirror and have a good belly laugh. For my patients who tell me they can't laugh on command, I tell them to fake it; pretty soon they are chuckling when they see how silly they look. And you don't have to laugh 'til you leak; just some grins and chuckles every day will also have healthy benefits."

Another way to build laughter into your day is to be more deliberate about being around people you really enjoy and steering clear of those you find emotionally draining. This is particularly important for the business traveler who finds himself or herself at a trade show or convention surrounded by friends and foes alike. You are in control, so carefully pick and choose whom you want to spend time with. Also, during times of stress, choose funny TV shows or movies and avoid those that are sad or violent.

Remember to keep things in perspective when it comes to stress. Clint Eastwood was quoted as saying, "I like people who take their work seriously, but don't take themselves too seriously." In addition to not taking yourself too seriously, remember the other two rules of stress management: 1. Don't sweat the small stuff, and 2. It's all small stuff.

Establish priorities. When you find you have a longer list of "to do" items than is reasonable, take time to decide which activities can wait. Decide which of those left on the action list you need to do now and get to it.

Talk things over. Often just the act of talking about

Bored? Need a mental break from your hectic schedule? Call (202) 456-2343 for a recorded message of the President's schedule for the day (Yes, that President).

If your flight options include a choice between two connections and the fares and service are equivalent, choose the one with the less-congested connecting airport. This reduces the risk of misconnecting.

a problem can have a healing effect by helping you put things in perspective. When you're on the road, remember to call home. Talking about things other than work is a good way to remember why you are on this business trip in the first place.

It can sometimes be difficult to relax when you are away from home and your body and mind are both reminding you of aches and pains and undone tasks. To get around this, try concentrating on something neutral—something that is neither good nor bad. This can help to clear your mind of the concerns of the moment, freeing it up for more relaxing activity.

For some of us, there is a more direct approach to relaxation. Instead of trying not to think about anything, imagine how you will feel when you are relaxed. Tension has some very specific effects on your body, so imagine the opposite effect.

When some people get stressed, their hands and feet become cooler as the body directs blood away from the extremities. Imagine that your hands and feet are nice and warm.

Other signs of relaxation are a relaxed jaw, a cool forehead, slow deep breathing, and a steady heartbeat.

It's a good idea to make a list of a few short sentences of how you will feel when you are relaxed. Keep the list in your briefcase or put in on your computer.

Short, simple sentences like "My hands are warm," are best. If you have just a few minutes, you can take this list out and read it to yourself. Find a quiet place and read the list ten times for best effect.

From Coping with Pain: Focus on Cancer. Vol 1, No. 3, Spring 1991. The KSF Group, New York.

Mental Vacations

Sometimes simply letting your mind wander or "go on vacation" will help reduce your stress. Here's a few mini-vacations you can do anywhere:

- Look to the west and watch the sunset.
- Take your shoes off and walk in the grass.
- Sit in a park on a sunny day and listen to the birds.
- Daydream about the beaches in Barbados while you're sitting beside the hotel swimming pool.
- Go to a pet store and stare at the fish in an aquarium.

Make a list of your own ideal mini-vacations and give your mind a break.

Finally, here's a way to relax when you're in a hurry. Find a comfortable chair in a relatively quiet spot. Put your feet on the floor, uncross your legs, and put your arms at your sides. Close your eyes and breathe in, saying to yourself, "I am…" then breathe out, saying, "…relaxed." Continue breathing slowly, silently repeating to yourself something like, "My hands are…" (breathe out) "warm." Or repeat the short sentences from your list above. Remind yourself that you feel at peace. This short "chair potato" routine takes only five minutes and you'll feel great afterward.

Music

"Life can't be all bad when for ten dollars you can buy all the Beethoven sonatas and listen to them for … years."
—William F. Buckley, Jr.

"Bach opens a vista to the universe. After experiencing him people feel there is meaning to life after all."
—Helmut Walcha

Towns to look for on your travels:

1. *Cut and Shoot, TX*
2. *Hell, MI*
3. *Santa Claus, AZ*
4. *Truth or Consequences, NM*
5. *Forty-Four, AK*
6. *Intercourse, PA*

Percentage of Americans who keep maps in their glove compartments: 50

Percentage who keep gloves in their glove compartments: 0

Music can be a wonderful aid to relaxation and stress management. Certain musical compositions have the power to transport us, others inspire us, and there are even some that are reputed to have healing power. Music can both relax and energize!

Here's a list of classical masterpieces and how they might affect us.

Bach, Double Concerto, or Violin Concertos 1 and 2: Stimulates joy, serenity, and a sense of radiance.

Bach, Brandenburg Concertos: There are many excellent recordings. The music offers a tremendous variety inspiring a full range of emotions from joy to sorrow to elation.

Mozart, Violin Concertos 3 and 5: Inspires magic, joy, and a sense of delight.

Pachelbel's Canon from Baroque Favorites: This music is soothing, full, rich, and life-supporting.

Chopin's Nocturnes: These are restful, dreamy, and peaceful. An excellent choice at bedtime.

Mahler, Symphony No. 4: This is full of delightful, energizing sounds.

Beethoven, Symphony No. 6 (The Pastoral): This piece of music inspires happiness and contentment.

Dvorak, Cello Concerto, and **Tchaikovsky,** Rococo Variations. Both of these are full of richness, earthiness, and warmth. Great to play if you are feeling homesick.

Mendelssohn, Violin Concertos, and the **Tchaikovsky,** Violin Concertos. These vibrant and passionate works promote feelings of health and well-being.

From The Fine Art of Recuperation: A Guide to Surviving and Thriving After Illness, Accident, or Surgery, by Regina Sara Ryan, Jeremy Tarcher/Putnam, Los Angeles, 1991.

Undoubtedly, you have your own list of favorites. Use them in your Walkman while in an airplane or play energizing selections in the car stereo while driving. But be careful not to get deeply involved in the music while you're driving.

Exercise

Exercise may be the closest thing there is to a "stress inoculation." Just as you can get a shot to build your body's immunity to certain germs, exercise is like taking a little dose of the stress germ to equip you to deal better with the stress bug when it comes to bite.

Exercisers not only burn off stress during each bout of physical activity, but because their bodies are stronger, they seem to be better able to tolerate the muscle tension, increased heart rates, and heavy respiration that can come with stressful events.

Chapter 2 describes a variety of exercises for the business traveler. All exercise is good for stress management, but when you don't have much time, here's a mini-list of some that are particularly convenient.

A stress-reliever walk: You can incorporate taking a walk into your business day by walking from one building to another instead of driving if distances are reasonable, or by using stairs instead of elevators. Instead of taking a coffee break, take a brisk walk around the building. Then get a cup of coffee to take back to work with you.

Park your car well away from your destination, and take a walk at lunchtime instead of sitting down for another half-hour in the cafeteria.

Back at your hotel, check out where the safest places to walk are (if you are in an urban setting where there may be a concern about crime.)

Sometimes you can simply stroll around the hotel perimeter or parking lot, but be sure to ask at the Front Desk if this is safe.

Bathroom ups and downs: While you're shaving or drying your hair, raise up and down on your toes for a count of 100. Do these

"Don't use cotton socks. These fibers absorb moisture and hold it against the skin, increasing the chances of blisters. Socks made of orlon or polypropylene (but not nylon) 'wick' perspiration away from the feet and provide better cushioning."

—Traveling Healthy

"After years of decline, Cadillac has returned as the top-seller in luxury cars, complete with extra length and fender skirts, outselling Mercedes and BMW by three to one."

—America By The Numbers

slowly to get maximum effect in the toes, feet, and calf muscles.

Stomach pumps: Another bathroom exercise for while you're shaving or drying your hair. Take a deep breath through your nose. Hold it in and tighten your stomach muscles for a count of 20. Do as many repetitions of this as your time allows.

The traffic tie-up: When you're in the car trapped in traffic, try some dynamic muscle tension exercises. Grab the steering wheel and push inward with both hands. Tighten your stomach muscles and add force from the inner arms to the shoulders. Repeat this until the traffic clears and you can continue on your way.

Leg stretches: If you are sitting at a desk or meeting table for hours, try to stretch your legs every hour or so. You can do this sitting down by straightening your legs out in front of you, holding them there for the count of 20, then relaxing them and replacing them on the floor. This increases blood circulation in the legs.

Turkey neck stretches: Turn your head as far to the left as you can. Then stretch it a bit farther to the left. Now do the same to the right. Repeat this several times to loosen the neck muscles and relieve strain.

Do the twist: Stand up with your feet together and pointed directly ahead of you. Twist your upper body and arms to the right and left, but keep your feet pointed forward. Repeat this motion until you feel your arms and hands relax.

Take a breather: Whenever you think of it, try to take a deep breath through your nose and hold it for as long as you can. Expel it completely through your mouth. Repeat this a few times and notice the feeling of renewal.

From Juliano, J., M.D., When Diabetes Complicates Your Life. CHRONIMED Publishing, Minneapolis: 1993.

One of the more interesting styles of exercising is called T'ai Chi Ch'uan.

This ancient art is a form of meditation in motion, with a superficial resemblance to the martial arts. It has a variety of aims and benefits, none of which is concerned with self-defense. These include:

- To experience a sense of balance, grace, and meaning that is inherent in movement.
- To deepen the breathing and clear the mind.
- To affect a complete fusion between movement and thought.
- To make you, by being in contact with the ground, more rooted and secure.
- To create a harmonious unity between body, mind, and spirit.

While it's outside the scope of this guide to teach the T'ai Chi program, we recommend that you look for one in your hometown or seek out a group in a local park in the places that you visit. Many mornings you'll find a group practicing this fine art in the fresh air, especially if your travel takes you to China.

With practice, the movements of T'ai Chi become balanced, smooth, and flowing, and they are wonderful stress relievers that you can easily do in your hotel room.

"A most useful stress-reducing technique is to allot at least 15 minutes a day for a quiet time by yourself. Simply relax, meditate, or pray."

—Minute Health Tips

Yoga is another form of stretching exercise that travels well. You don't need much space and it is a very quiet form of stress-relieving activity. Alternate nostril breathing has a tranquilizing effect on the mind. Try:

1. Sitting in the lotus position (that is straight on the floor with your knees bent and your ankles crossed), or simply with your back straight, close your eyes and mouth.

2. Shut your right nostril by pressing the side with the right thumb. Keep the next two fingers bent and the last two fingers together and straight. Breathe in through the left nostril until the lungs are comfortably filled.

3. Close the nose for a few seconds, using the last two fingers to press the left nostril.

4. Release the right nostril and exhale slowly, then breathe in on the right to fill the lungs. Again close the nose, this time reapplying the thumb. Hold for a few seconds. Release the left nostril, breathe out slowly, and immediately breathe in again.

5. Repeat the entire sequence five times, finishing with the final out-breath on the left side.

Yoga exercises center around stretching and all start from a central standing position. In this position, you:

1. Allow your face to relax into a neutral expression and feel your throat loosen.

2. Imagine the back of your neck is extending so your chin tucks in.

3. Relax your shoulders until they slope slightly and your arms hang limply. As the shoulders incline backward, your chest comes forward.

4. Stretch your spine and feel yourself "grow" several inches.

5. Pull your stomach in, without constricting breathing.

6. Keep your feet together but your weight evenly distributed.

Maintaining this position for a few minutes helps improve your posture and so prevents physical and mental fatigue.

With your weight evenly distributed, your spine stretched, your stomach taut, and your shoulders relaxed, your body assumes its natural position. This frees the body from strain and gives a feeling of heightened awareness.

Another pose is called the "corpse pose." It can be the energizer you need if you are short of sleep or feeling tense. Lie on your back, with your feet in a V-shape, your arms by your sides. With your eyes closed, breathe in for a count of six, hold for three, breathe out for six, and hold for three.

Repeat this cycle for about 10 minutes, then stretch and get up. Other yoga stretches that help manage stress are:

The triangle pose: Place your feet more than hip width apart with your left foot at right angles to your right. Put your left hand on your left leg and stretch your right hand up as you inhale. As you exhale, let your left hand slide down your leg until you reach your ankle. Look up to the right hand as you breathe in this position. Hold this stretch for one minute, then repeat it on the other side. Do this three times.

The knee-hug pose: Standing erect, focus your eyes on a stationary object in front of you. Lift your right knee into your chest and grasp the knee with both hands. Keep your ribs lifted out of your waist. Hold this for one minute, then repeat on the other side. (If you are doing this for the first time, be sure to stand near a wall in case you feel wobbly on one leg.)

The full-body stretch: Lie face down, arms stretched above your head. As you inhale, stretch your right arm and leg as far as possible away from each other, tucking your pelvis forward into the floor. Exhale as you release. Repeat three times on each side.

There are many other more exotic poses in yoga and many of the movements are meant to be performed in a series. The one featured on the next page is called "The Sun Salutation," and is performed in ten steps.

Stress Management Exercises

The series is designed to be performed at sunrise when the air is fresh and energizing. No matter what your schedule, the Sun exercises will help restore your vitality, increase and maintain flexibility, and tone your muscles. Here's how to do this series:

1. Stand erect, balanced on the soles of your feet, palms together. Feel the top of your head connected to the ceiling.

2. Inhale, stretching your arms high, and bend back. Keep your arms close to your ears, and don't let your head hang back. Focus on stretching through the front of your body; if you feel a pinch in your lower back, you are bending too far.

3. As you exhale, bend forward, knees slightly bent. Place your fingertips beside your toes.

4. Inhale, extend your left leg back, your left knee on the floor, your chest and head lifted.

5. Hold your breath as you extend your left leg back into a "push up" position, and support yourself with your abdominal muscles.

6. Exhale as you bend your knees to the floor, chest down between your hands, chin on the floor.

7. Inhale as you slide your chest forward, lifting your head and chest up, your eyes looking straight ahead. If you have any pain in your back, bend your elbows more and make sure your shoulders are pressed down, away from your ears.

8. Curl your toes under, and as you exhale, push back on your heels; your buttocks are thrust into the air, and your head is down.

9. Inhale and slide your left foot forward between your hands, your right knee on the floor, your head and chest lifted.

10. Exhale and slide your left foot forward, keeping your feet together.

Inhale and slowly roll up, stretch up and bend back as in step 2. Exhale and return to the start position.

You can do this series in the evenings after you return from your work and before you go out for dinner. It will leave you feeling relaxed and refreshed.

A Five-Day Stress Management Plan

Here's a plan for systematic stress reduction. Use this in conjunction with your dine-around and exercise programs for total well-being management during your travels.

DAY ONE

Early Morning

Right after you've answered your wake-up call and just before you get out of bed, use self-talk to tell yourself, "Good morning." While you're feeling relaxed from sleep, preview the events of the coming day and see yourself handling every challenge in a positive and efficient manner. Remind yourself of your decision to stay healthy.

Mid-Afternoon

Sometime around 2 or 2:30, sneak away from whatever you're doing and find a quiet spot. This might be a bathroom, or perhaps a lounge. Maybe the cafeteria is empty. Be resourceful and find a quiet place.

Sit down with your feet on the floor. You don't even need to close your eyes if you're not comfortable doing so. Take 10 minutes to tell your body to relax. Congratulate yourself on how well you're handling the day's problems. Use self-talk to give yourself positive messages that are specific to your situation such as the following, but be sure to make your own.

When selecting a flight, remember that a departure early in the day is less likely to be delayed than a later flight, due to "ripple" effects throughout the day. If you book the last flight of the day, you could get stuck overnight.

1. "I'm really contributing to that meeting. I'll go back and continue to toss out my best ideas."

2. "I'm proud that I'm staying so calm even though Sam is being so confrontational. I'll get my point across in my own quiet, matter-of-fact way."

Early Evening
Sometime around 6 p.m., and just before dinner, take time for the complete 15 to 20 minute muscle relaxation session on page 68. Lie down on the bed in your hotel room and tense and relax all the muscle sets. You'll soon feel refreshed and ready for a night on the town.

Bedtime
Use a guided imagery tape to relax and get ready for sleep. If you fall asleep before it is over, don't worry. Your Walkman will turn off by itself.

DAY TWO

Early Morning
For your personal wake-up message, use self-talk to tell yourself that it's a great morning. You feel rested and ready to go. Before you get out of bed, preview your day's events as on Day One and tell yourself that you'll do a great job and enjoy handling the tasks at hand.

Noon
Take a 10-minute walk around the block to reduce any stress you might be feeling. Remind yourself that your utmost concern is your personal health and well-being.

Early Evening
Lie down for 20 minutes in your hotel room and relax. Do a muscle relaxation meditation or use a guided imagery tape and isolate yourself completely from your work-day worries.

Bedtime
Try relaxing by watching television tonight. Find something amusing, but not too absorbing. Get sleepy with

humor and build up your supply of endorphins for tomorrow.

DAY THREE

Early Morning

Right after the alarm goes off, try thinking "Oh good! It's morning. I feel great. I'm ready to get up, right after I preview my day."

Preview the day's events as on previous mornings and see yourself handling all of them efficiently and with good humor.

Midday

Stop by a deli and get yourself a healthy box lunch. Take it to a park and enjoy it in the ambience of the natural world. Remind yourself to stay in balance and observe the harmony and beauty of nature. Note the grace and elegance of a tree. Look at the intricate patterns of the feathers on a bird. Marvel at the blueness of the sky and the warmth of the sun.

Before you leave the park and return to work, remind yourself that you belong in this beautiful universe and that you are working toward being in complete harmony with your world.

Early Evening

Just before dinner, at around 6 p.m., do a 15- to 20-minute meditation session of your choice.

Bedtime

Reread one of the Guided Imagery Meditations in this book on pages 70 and 72. Listen to the most relaxing music tape of your choice while you do. As you drift off to sleep, congratulate yourself for a successful day and tell yourself that you are looking forward to tomorrow.

DAY FOUR

Early Morning

After the wake-up call, tell yourself, "I've had another restful night. I'm ready to go." Then preview the day's events as on previous mornings. See yourself succeeding at everything.

Mid-Afternoon

When everyone else goes to the coffee machine, take a 10-minute break to go someplace quiet and tell yourself that you have chosen to be healthy. Consider this tip from *The One Minute Manager:*

It take four things to maintain a sense of balance:

- *Autonomy:* The feeling of being in control. You have the power to choose to be healthy and happy.

- *Connectedness:* The feeling of security from having strong, positive relationships at home, at work, and in the community.

- *Perspective:* The feeling that your life has a purpose, a direction, and the feeling of passion that helps you pursue your goals with enthusiasm.

- *Tone:* The positive feeling you have about your body, your energy level, your physical well-being, and your appearance.

From: Blanchard, K., Ph.D., Edington, D.W., Ph.D., and Blanchard, M., Ph.D., The One Minute Manager Gets Fit; William Morrow and Company, Inc. New York: 1986.

Early Evening

When you return to your hotel, lie down and do a 15- to 20-minute meditation. If you have time, do 10 minutes of yoga stretches after you get up.

Bedtime

Play your favorite music on your Walkman. Find something uplifting and inspiring to read and tell yourself to have a rest-filled night.

DAY FIVE

Early Morning

Greet the day with a personal good morning message, specific to the day's circumstance. That might be: "I'm happy that I'm on my way home this morning," or "What a great morning, I'll take part of this day off." Preview your day's events, paying particular attention to any enjoyable events you have to look forward to.

Midday

Take 10 minutes before lunch to sit quietly and do the "Short Form" meditation on page 69. Relax, restore your perspective, and remind yourself that you are doing a great job.

Early Evening

Assuming that you are using the Five-Day Plan for a Monday to Friday trip, you could well be on your way home by now. If you're in a plane, your car, or on a train, use your imagination and invent your own imagery for relaxation. Find a mental place you like to go and then spend some time there, just resting and relaxing. Congratulate yourself on the completion of a successful week.

Please note: If you are driving, this is not the relaxation exercise for you. Refer to the exercises found earlier in this chapter and put some calming music on the car radio.

Bedtime

If you're one of the lucky business travelers, you might be home in your own bed by now. And if your spouse or companion is with you, you don't need any tips for stress relief from us.

But, if you're still on the road, or if you're having trouble relaxing after a travel day filled with hassles, here's a count-down meditation to help. Counting backwards is a common relaxation technique that helps many people get quiet and sleepy.

Lie down and close your eyes. Begin counting backwards from 50. Time each count to match your breathing: after you exhale, notice that you don't have to breathe in again immediately. Just rest for a few seconds. For some people this may be only a few seconds, but for others it may be as long as 20 seconds. During this peaceful time when the lungs have paused and the body is still, count one number for each cycle of breathing in and out.

As you practice counting these breaths, it's okay to lose track of the number. When this occurs, simply resume counting from whatever number you can remember and keep going. If you reach number one and are still wide awake, begin counting backwards again, this time starting with number 100.

Begin to be aware of how long your inhale-exhale cycles are. Do they lengthen as you begin to get more and more relaxed? Try to notice the other signs of relaxation: Are your palms warm? Is your forehead cool?

Most people never complete this exercise. Take all the time you need to develop your relaxation response and switch to a guided imagery tape if you need more help. If you find sleep just will not come, then try distracting yourself with television. Be sure you find something uplifting, though, since violence and noise will produce the opposite effects and keep you awake even longer.

Use Your ComputerTo Help You Manage Stress

Many of us on the road today are carrying our business lives in our lap-top computers. Here are some tips for how to incorporate your computer into a stress management program:

1. Create a subdirectory called "ME."

2. In this subdirectory, create a file called "INSPIRE," and type the following list of messages:

"Be thankful for the troubles of your job. They provide about half your income, because if it were not for the things that go wrong, the difficult people you have to deal with, and the problems and unpleasantness of your working day, someone could be found to handle your job for half of what you are being paid.

"It takes intelligence, resourcefulness, patience, tact, and courage to meet the troubles of any job. That is why you hold your present job. If all of us would start to look for more troubles and learn to handle them cheerfully and with good judgment as opportunities rather than irritation, we would find ourselves getting ahead at a surprising rate. For it is a fact that there are plenty of big jobs waiting for those who aren't afraid of the troubles connected with them."

(From: The Benefits of Trouble by The Rev. John Wesley Ford)

"The mind ought sometimes to be amused, that it may the better return to thought, and to itself."
—Phaedrus (5th Century B.C.)

"Through appreciation we make the excellence in others our own property."
—Voltaire

Hold fast to dreams
For if Dreams die
Life is a broken-winged bird
That cannot fly.

Hold fast to dreams
For when Dreams go
Life is a barren field
Frozen with snow.
—Langston Hughes

"We must try to take life moment by moment. The actual present is usually pretty tolerable...if only we refrain from adding to its burden that of the past and the future...."
—C.S. Lewis

"If you use a lap top computer on airplanes, keep your seat back upright, sit straight, and place magazines and your briefcase under the computer to raise the screen to eye level. This helps prevent neck strain and backaches."

—Traveling Healthy

"Perseverance is not a long race; it is many short races one after another."
—Walter Elliot

"To reach port...we must sail, sometimes with the wind and sometimes against it, but we must sail, not drift or lie at anchor."
—Oliver Wendell Holmes

"Life is not a matter of holding good cards. It's playing a poor hand well."
—Robert Louis Stevenson

"He who has a why to live can bear almost any how."
—Friedrich Nietzsche

"Productivity can be realized if you believe in the future, if you believe that today is going to be better than yesterday and tomorrow is going to be better than today...that is expressed in Japan in having a meaningful purpose for work and for living."
—Ichiro Shioji (in *Automotive News*)

"The greatest revolution of our generation is the discovery that human beings, by changing the inner attitudes of their minds, can change the outer aspects of their lives."
—William James

"No one can make you feel inferior without your consent."
—Eleanor Roosevelt

"Belief is the most powerful motivator of them all. You will not be motivated to do anything unless you believe that it will lead to a positive outcome."
—Catherine Feste (in *The Physician Within*)

"A problem well stated is a problem half-solved."
—Charles F. Kettering

"When we treat a man as he is, we make him worse than he is. When we treat him as if he already were what he potentially could be, we make him what he should be."
—Goethe

"We are not at our best perched at the summit; we are climbers, at our best when the way is steep."
—John W. Gardner

(Quotes from Feste, C. The Physician Within; CHRONIMED Publishing, Minneapolis: 1993.)

3. Create another file called "Jokes." Use this file to keep a record of any good jokes you hear on the road, and fill it with your personal favorites. Here are 10 of our favorites to get you started:

- Mary returned from a trip totally exhausted. Her husband asked what had happened. She said, "My computer went down and I had to think all week."

- You know your company is in trouble when you have to conduct your inventory in the purchasing agent's garage.

- Do you suppose that when ministers make mistakes they are known as clerical errors?

- An executive was dictating his will. "I want my older son to get a hundred thousand dollars," he started. "Put my younger son down for seventy-five thousand. And my twin daughters should have a quarter of a million each."

  His attorney seemed puzzled and asked, "Where is all this money coming from?"

  The executive said, "Let them work for it like I did."

- We know an executive who's got a lot of problems. A major one came up yesterday, but he can't fit it into his schedule for worrying until next week."

- An employee went in to his boss and asked for a raise, saying, "I'm doing the work of three people."

  The boss said, "Okay, tell me the names of the other two and I'll fire them."

"Experience is the name everyone gives to their mistakes."
Oscar Wilde

"Cradling a telephone between your neck and shoulder, a common way of holding a car phone, can cause neck and back strain, says the Comprehensive Spine Center in Los Angeles."

—Traveling Healthy

- "These really are good times, but only a few people know about it." — quoted from Henry Ford
- A little boy returned from his first experience in church and was asked how it went. He said, "The music and singing were nice, but the commercial was too long."
- My job is so stressful, my computer has an ulcer.
- Noah was the greatest banker who ever lived. He floated an entire company when the whole world was in liquidation.

A final humorous note: Remember that if you work hard and every year you put away ten thousand dollars for a rainy day, if it doesn't rain, you're stuck with fifty thousand dollars at the end of five years.

4. Set the alarm clock on your computer to 2 p.m. to remind you to take a stress-relief break. Read the notes in your ME file just before leaving your desk.

5. For DOS users, use the edit command and go to your AUTOEXEC.BAT file. On the line where you see the word "PROMPT," insert the following message: "Hi there. Did you read your ME files today?" This message goes between the word PROMPT and any other characters on that line. Save the AUTOEXEC.BAT file. The next time your C: prompt appears on your screen, the handy reminder will also appear. (You will want to be sure you have backed-up your AUTOEXEC.BAT before you edit the file.)

6. Go into your ME subdirectory and create another file called: CHKLST. In your CHKLST file, type the following:

Checklist of Personal Diet, Exercise, and Stress Management Goals

Respond with true or false answers to the following:

❑ Today I started my day feeling rested.

❑ I remembered to give myself positive reinforcement as I previewed my day's events.

❑ I found the time to participate in healthful exercise.

❑ I ate breakfast per my Five-Day plan.

❑ I took some time to remind myself that I have autonomy and I choose to be healthy and happy.

❑ I ate a healthful lunch.

❑ I remembered to take a stress management break and found 10 minutes during my day to relax.

❑ I read my ME files to regain my perspective.

❑ I supported my colleagues and felt supported by them.

❑ I will find (or found) the time to do a complete 20-minute muscle relaxation or guided imagery meditation as a way to help my body regain strength after the day's stressful events.

❑ I will eat (or have eaten) a healthful dinner that is consistent with my health and nutrition goals.

❑ I will remember (or have remembered) to do something relaxing at bedtime to soothe my spirits and enable me to get a good night's rest.

At the end of your computing day, read your CHKLST file and congratulate yourself for every TRUE answer.

Power down and have a good evening.

"We must try to take life moment by moment. The actual present is usually pretty tolerable...."

4

HEALTH CONCERNS

It's amazing how seemingly insignificant things can affect your health when you are traveling. The hotel pillow, the late-night snack, or even television programs can throw your body off balance.

Stress and illness will directly affect your work when you are on the road and can seriously impact how much you will enjoy the trip. But there are many things that can be done to maintain or improve your health on the road. And it all starts with getting a good night's rest.

Sleeplessness

Dr. Dale Anderson, the "humor doctor" referred to earlier, says having difficulty going to sleep is similar to when you turn the ignition off and the motor keeps running. The "run on" depends on the fuel, timing, conditioning, and many other commonly overlooked factors that are individually small but collectively big.

"We may be able to tolerate some adverse factors, but one additional may be the 'drop that causes the boat to sink,'" says Dr. Anderson. A tired body—physically and mentally—does not allow the normal stress- and illness-fighting mechanisms to work properly. The key is getting the proper rest.

There are many barriers to good sleep, and eliminating as many as possible will improve your chances for a restful night. You should avoid:

To improve sleep, avoid...

1. Caffeine at least 6 hours before bedtime (coffee, tea, cola or other caffeine-containing soft drinks and unnecessary medications)
2. Chocolate

To improve sleep, avoid...

3. Nasal sprays
4. Stomach relaxants
5. Alcohol
6. High sugar intake at bedtime
7. Sodium
8. Late dinners
9. Dehydration (environmental and within the body)
10. Exercising too close to bedtime. (Although this raises endorphins, which is good, exercise also raises the body's metabolism for several hours making it more difficult to "slow" the body down for sleep.)
11. Clock watching—Recent studies have shown that people with lighted clocks at bedside spend a significant amount of time "evaluating" how well they are sleeping. Those who didn't know the time all night and expected only to be awakened at a given signal rested much better than those who evaluated their sleep "success" by watching the clock.
12. Smoking—nicotine is a stimulant.
13. Watching the Evening News—The old saying, "No news is good news," is very true when it comes to sleep. The 10 o'clock news is not "user friendly." It's full of stories about the latest war, murder, robbery, and accident, which do nothing to act as a sleep-inducing lullaby.

Just as there are things you should avoid, there are things you can do to enhance a good night's sleep:

To enhance a good night's sleep

- *Raise your endorphins,* which reduce pain, relax muscles, suppress the appetite, and create the "good feeling" of optimism, hope, happiness, joy, and so forth. This can be done by:

—Taking a hot bath
—Making friendly "connections" by calling home, gazing at a family picture, or saying a prayer
—Laughing with a good book or watching TV comedy
—Physical conditioning (not too close to bedtime)

- *Rearrange the room.* Most of the accidents that occur in a "strange" room are because of falling or tripping over furniture or "travel debris." Also, move the telephone, clock radio, and so forth close to the bed so you will not have to make a desperate, groping lunge to awaken.

- *Bring nightlights* to permit you to "navigate" a room without having to turn on a bright light, which will trigger "wake up" messages in the body.

- *Request a different pillow.* Often hotel management will have a more comfortable one.

- *Raise the head of the bed* by placing extra pillows under the mattress.

- *Control noise* by:

—Requesting a room on the tenth floor or above if on the street-side of the hotel
—Getting a room away from the elevator or stairways
—Using "soft" ear plugs

- *Try to get a room with an east or south exposure* to get more morning sun, making it easier to wake up in the morning and cooler at night than a west exposure.

- *Keep the room at 65 degrees* in the afternoon and night.

Thomas G. Welch, M.D., author of *Minute Health Tips,* suggests:

- Read a book until your eyes get very heavy.

- Focus on an object on the ceiling and try to "move it" with your eyes. This is fatiguing for your eyes and might help to promote sleep.

- Don't fight it! You can't force sleep; you simply have to relax and let it happen.

- If you must eat, have some low-fat milk or bananas. They contain a substance called tryptophan which seems to help promote relaxation and sleep.

The dry conditions in planes can irritate the eyes. Use saline eye drops before, during, and after the flight.

A final note on sleeplessness, use the countdown exercise on page 89 as a way of helping you step away from whatever has kept your engine running. And it's perfectly okay to count sheep, unless, of course, you are a shepherd.

Health Concerns on a Plane

Many of us routinely take to the air on our business trips. Occasionally, we might encounter some flight-related discomforts, especially when we travel long distances.

Dr. Thomas Welch tells us that prolonged sitting in an airplane seat may cause swelling of the feet and can even lead to blood clots in the lower leg. This is caused by poor blood circulation due to inactivity and lack of muscle movement. It can affect people of all ages, so if you're going on a long flight, try this:

- Flex your toes upward and hold for a count of 10, then put them down. Do this about eight times every 30 minutes. This will improve muscle activity and circulation. Of course, getting up and walking around will also help.

Ear Problems

According to a report by the Airport Operators Council International, Inc., ear problems are the most common medical complaint of airplane travelers. Many people experience a sensation of fullness in the ears or popping when in flight. The following tips can help equalize the pressure in the middle ear:

1. Swallow frequently when you are in flight, especially before descent. Chewing gum or allowing mints to melt in your mouth will create a need for you to swallow more often.

2. Avoid sleeping during descent because you may not swallow often enough to keep up with pressure changes.

Valsalva Maneuver

3. If yawning or swallowing is not effective, use the "Valsalva maneuver":

—Pinch your nostrils shut.
—Breathe in a mouthful of air.
—Using only cheek and throat muscles, create pressure

and force the air into the back of your nose as if you were trying to blow your thumb and fingers off your nostrils.

—Be gentle and blow in short successive attempts. When you hear or feel a pop in your ears, you have succeeded.

—Never use force from your chest (lungs) or abdomen (diaphragm) because that can create pressures that are too intense.

If you have a bad cold, sinus infection, earache, or allergy attack, postpone the airplane trip if at all possible. If you have a stuffy nose before boarding, use a decongestant or nasal spray an hour before take-off and an hour before landing. This will shrink the membranes in the nose that connect with the ears, allowing the ears to release the pressure more easily.

4. Decongestant tablets and sprays should be avoided by persons with heart disease, high blood pressure, irregular heart rhythms, thyroid diseases, or excessive nervousness. Pregnant women should consult their physicians first before using these over-the-counter medications. You should also avoid driving after using a decongestant. Altitude, jet lag, fatigue, and decongestants can have a cumulative effect on drowsiness.

5. After landing you may continue the pressure equalizing techniques, but if your ears fail to open or pain persists, seek the help of a physician who has experience in the care of ear disorders.

Motion or Air Sickness

If your business trip includes a half-day cruise, imagine your disappointment (and discomfort) if you get seasick after only one hour. Or suppose you leave home and get car sick on your way to the airport, not to mention how sick you would feel once you're airborne. Motion sickness can really spoil the travel part of business travel.

Now there's a simple patch to help handle this common problem. It's called *Transderm Scōp,* and it contains scopolamine, which has been known for years as an effective aid for seasickness. But its use was limited by

If you are prone to motion sickness, request a seat over the wing on the right side of the plane. Most flight patterns turn left, so passengers on the right side aren't swung around as much.

troublesome side effects experienced after it was taken orally. These occur less with the patch.

The patch, a small, flesh-colored, adhesive patch about the size of a dime, is applied to an area of intact skin, like behind the ear. The patch continuously releases a measured amount of medication and has been shown to be more effective than antihistamines.

The patch has even been used by astronauts in outer space. And unlike *Dramamine* and other over-the-counter motion-sickness remedies, the patch generally does not make you drowsy. However, sometimes people experience withdrawal after they stop using the patches. The following guidelines may help you avoid this:

1. Leave the patch on for two days instead of the recommended three.

2. Since scopolamine is present in the urine for at least two days after a patch is removed, wait a day or two before putting on a second fresh one.

Remember that the patch is for use on adults only. If you have glaucoma, an enlarged prostate, trouble with your urinary bladder, or pyloric obstruction (a narrowing between the stomach and small intestines that causes vomiting), the patch is not for you. It also is not recommended for pregnant or nursing women.

Side effects may occur not only after you remove the patch, but while you're wearing it as well. The most frequent is dryness of the mouth, but the package insert accompanying the drug says it can cause restlessness, giddiness, temporary confusion, drowsiness, and blurred vision. Remove the patch immediately if you experience any of these. If the side effects don't resolve within a day, see a doctor.

From Rosenfeld, I. Modern Prevention, The New Medicine; Linden Press/Simon and Schuster, New York: 1986.

Finally, don't forget to wash your hands and dry them thoroughly before and after you apply the patch. Scopolamine will temporarily blur vision if it gets in your eyes. And always clean the area of skin to which you affix it. You don't want to absorb any impurities with the drug. Consult your doctor if you have any concerns about your specific medical condition or situation.

Altitude Sickness

People who ascend rapidly to altitudes over 6,000 feet sometimes get altitude or acute mountain sickness. Symptoms include headache, dizziness, fatigue, breathlessness, insomnia, and loss of appetite. The headache is throbbing, made worse by lying down, and it is exacerbated by exercise and by alcohol.

If your destination is in the mountains and you have heart or lung problems, you'll want to take it easy once you arrive. There are a few simple rules that will help prevent altitude sickness:

1. After your arrival in a mountain destination, avoid any vigorous activity for 24 to 48 hours.

2. Carry some acetazolamide (a prescription known as Diamox) in 250 mg. strength if you think you are susceptible or if you have suffered before. Diamox is a diuretic widely used in the treatment of glaucoma that stimulates deep breathing. Take three tablets the day you arrive and then two a day for the next three days. You should have no problems tolerating this medication in such small doses, but be prepared to empty your bladder frequently.

3. Avoid all alcohol for the first two days and drink lots of water.

4. Eat lightly, mostly carbohydrates, rather than fat or protein.

5. Do not take sedatives or tranquilizers. Your brain, working with less oxygen at high altitudes, doesn't do well with further depression of its functions.

"There is only one guaranteed way to prevent seasickness. An old English sailor's proverb says, 'Sit on the shady side of an old brick church in the country and never, never go to the sea.'"

—Traveling Healthy

Jet Lag

You can reduce the effects of jet lag by being physically fit, by not smoking, and, according to some, by paying attention to your diet.

Jet lag is a form of stress that you should manage just like you manage other stress in your life. Here are some tips:

1. Don't drink too much alcohol—Alcohol is a depressant drug. It can cause nervous stimulation and restlessness, interfering with sleep and well-being.

2. Don't drink too much coffee—Caffeine is a weak diuretic that may cause increased urination and mild fluid loss. Excess caffeine my cause overstimulation, nervousness, anxiety, tremors, and insomnia.

3. Do drink water—lots of it. You may be already dehydrated at the start of the flight due to disrupted eating and drinking patterns prior to departure. Breathing dry cabin air will increase this dehydration unless you drink fluids.

Water is the best anti-jet lag diet known. You should force fluids before and during your travel. Because your body's thirst mechanism does not warn you about dehydration, you need to drink on a regular basis even though you don't feel thirsty.

Resetting the Body's Clock

If water alone doesn't do the trick, the Argonne National Laboratory (one of the research centers in energy and basic sciences of the U.S. Department of Energy) offers a plan to reset the body's clock, claiming that it's not just the lack of sleep that causes jet lag. These scientists say their plan helps to minimize the problems of jet lag by resetting the body's biological rhythm quickly.

Basically, they suggest that you start preparing yourself three days before you leave. On that day, you "feast," on high-protein fare like meat, eggs, fish, high-protein cereals, and green beans. You restrict coffee between 3 and 5 p.m., then have a dinner of lots of carbohydrates, like pasta without meatballs, potatoes, starchy vegetables, and sweet desserts that help you sleep. The next day you fast, that is you limit your calorie intake, eating small salads, light soups, unbuttered toast, a little fruit, and a glass of juice. Again no coffee between 2 and 5 p.m. On day three, you feast again.

On the day of departure, you fast. If you are going west, like from New York to Los Angeles, you only fast half a day. Any coffee you drink that day should be consumed before noon. If you go east, however, you fast all day, and any coffee you drink should be taken only between 6 and 11 p.m. On the plane, you sleep all you can, and you try not to have any alcohol, even if it's free.

On the day of arrival, wake up and have a high-protein breakfast when it's 7 a.m. at your destination. Then stay awake and read or walk about the plane as much as you can. Once you've landed, follow the meal pattern in the city you're visiting. Go to bed early in the evening on arrival day, but not as soon as you're on the ground. The next day you'll feel adjusted. While this may sound a little complicated, it really isn't and if you travel a lot, it might be worth trying.

Travel Fatigue

Travel can be exhausting, as the frequent business traveler can tell you. In addition to the anti-jet lag steps suggested above, you'll want to be sure to get sufficient rest once you've arrived. On arrival day, to help combat travel fatigue, be sure to pack a swimsuit. More and more hotels offer a jacuzzi hot tub in which to relax. See Chapter 3 on stress relief for other relaxation techniques.

Loneliness

Bring work or a magazine to a restaurant if you are dining alone, or ask another single diner to join you. Combat that feeling of loneliness by introducing yourself to other guests at your hotel. You may meet someone who will be interested in dining with you or touring the city with you. You never know if you don't reach out. Use good judgment or ask your hotel concierge for assistance in identifying other solo travelers.

"Turbulence is most common in winter, generally when warm and cold air masses collide. Sometimes it occurs without warning and can be violent. Each year dozens of people are injured aboard US airlines, sometimes by being thrown against the ceiling. Wear seatbelts."

—Traveling Healthy

Bring leisure-time materials or activities like books to read, embroidery projects, or crossword puzzle books. Use free time to do mini-projects you don't have time for at home. Pamper yourself with long bathtub soaks or sing at the top of your voice in the shower. Watch movies on TV. Many hotels have some of the cable channels that feature old movies, and others have movie choices that you can select from your room for personal viewing on your schedule. Some of the better hotels now feature VCRs and have a tape library in the lobby where with a single swipe of your American Express card you can watch as many tapes as you can in a 24-hour period for only one nominal charge.

The radio is another source of entertainment. Music, talk shows, and even "A Prairie Home Companion" on American Public Radio are all available for your listening pleasure.

If you spend long hours in the car, you'll want to check out Books on Tape. You can listen to the latest in fiction or fact using your car's tape player and rental tapes from this California company whose aim is to make listening a pleasure and a convenience. Once you have finished a tape, just put it back in the mailing container and drop it in any mailbox. They even pay the return postage. Contact them at: (800) 626-3333.

Another company, Ride With Me, sells audio cassettes that relate the history, legends, geography, and music of the countryside along certain highway routes. For instance, "The Mount Vernon Story" tells little known stories of George and Martha Washington. For more information, call (800) 752-3195.

Indigestion and Other Inconveniences

Acid indigestion, or heartburn, and a sour stomach can dampen your enthusiasm for eating out. When you're on the road, eating out may be the norm. So, if you are uncomfortable after eating too much salsa on your nachos, or if you had more alcohol than your system could handle, here are some tips for handling stomach aches and heartburn.

Over-the-counter antacids, such as *Rolaids, Gelusil,* or *Tums,* neutralize excess gastric acids and are helpful in relieving heartburn and minor indigestion. Although there are scores of antacids on the market, all contain one or more of four active ingredients: sodium bicarbonate, calcium carbonate, magnesium salts, and aluminum salts. If you are traveling where none of the over-the-counter tablets you recognize are available and the ones you packed in your travel kit are gone, read the labels to see if what is available contains at least one of these ingredients.

Sodium bicarbonate is rapid acting but offers only short-term relief. Calcium carbonate is also fast-acting, but it can cause constipation. Aluminum and magnesium preparations are slower acting but longer lasting. Magnesium antacids, if overused, can cause diarrhea, however, and aluminum-based ones, constipation. None of these products should be taken indiscriminately.

Remedies for Heartburn and Simple Indigestion

In addition to antacids, here are some other remedies for heartburn and simple indigestion:

- Avoid caffeine, alcohol, aspirin, fatty or highly acidic foods, or any food you suspect contributes to the problem.
- Don't wear tight clothing, particularly around your waist.
- To keep stomach acids flowing in the right direction while you sleep, place a hard-cover book, bricks, or whatever between the mattress and box spring to elevate the head of your bed 4 to 6 inches. The hotel staff can usually help find a wedge if you need one.
- Don't lie down immediately after eating.
- If stress triggers your heartburn or indigestion, try to relax, especially before you eat.

Stomach Upset

If your stomach upset also includes some bowel upset, it could be the result of a viral infection. Check the following section on diarrhea. If you have some vomiting, be aware that this is your body's reaction to eating infected food. Your greatest concern in recovering from vomiting or diarrhea is to prevent dehydration, so it's important to drink plenty of fluids. Frequent, small sips of clear liquids should do the job. Here are four steps for a prompt recovery:

- Let your stomach rest. This means you should put nothing in your stomach when you're feeling nauseated; gradually add liquids as the nausea subsides.

- Stay on clear liquids for the first full day. Try water, cracked ice, bouillon, gelatin, or soda with the fizz gone flat, sipping a little at a time throughout the day. International travelers should be wary of water and ice. Read more about food and water safety on page 113.

- Add bland foods on the second day. Choose foods like bananas, rice, applesauce, unbuttered toast, clear soup, dry crackers, or breakfast cereals without milk. Eat these in small amounts.

- Get plenty of rest. If your stomach upset is the flu, it's best to be lazy until it passes.

From Terry, P.E., Ph.D., and Kind, A.C., M.D., F.A.C.P. It's Your Body; CHRONIMED Publishing; Minneapolis: 1992.

Travelers' Diarrhea

Run-of-the-mill gastroenteritis, (also known as "turista," the "Aztec Two-Step," "Montezuma's Revenge," or "Dehli Belly") which afflicts tourists is usually more of a nuisance than a serious threat. It is almost always due to *Escherichia coli* (E. coli), a bacterium normally present in the gut. Strains of this organism vary from country to country, and sometimes from region to region within a country. If you pick up a different form of E. coli, you may have some watery diarrhea and abdominal cramps for a couple of days.

Loperamide, which is available over the counter as Imodium AD, provides relief from mild diarrhea. This comes in tablets or liquid form, and was a recommendation for inclusion in your travel kit. Imodium has a rapid and direct effect on the bowel and has few side effects. Adequate replacement of fluids is also essential. Except for eliminating dairy products, you shouldn't need to make any special dietary changes if your diarrhea is mild.

Guidelines For Preventing Traveler's Diarrhea

Rule 1: Pay careful attention to what you eat and drink.

Rule 2: Wash your hands with soap and water before eating to prevent diarrhea-causing bacteria or parasites from your hands to get onto your food.

Rule 3: Use Pepto-Bismol tablets prophylactically in a dosage of two tablets, four times daily, if you think you are at risk. Pepto-Bismol has been shown to eliminate certain types of bacteria from the stomach and intestine. The tablets are better than the liquid form since you would need to consume a bottle a day to have the same effect as the eight tablets daily. Imodium is also effective.

NOTE: If you are taking aspirin regularly for medical reasons and notice ringing in the ears or a tendency toward easy bruising, discontinue the Pepto-Bismol. It contains salicylate, just as aspirin does, and you could be getting too much. If you are taking Coumadin or some other anticoagulant, you might experience bleeding. Pepto-Bismol has the salicylate content of about one adult aspirin tablet. Check with your doctor about this if you have any chronic medical condition for which you are taking medication.

Rule 4. Take antibiotics. There is some evidence that taking an antibiotic along with Imodium at the onset of diarrhea is very effective. This is something to discuss with your doctor if you are traveling to Mexico,

"Most drugs—particularly tranquilizers and sedatives—have more potency at high altitudes . . . . Ask your physician about it, but don't expect a precise answer since the effect is hard to quantify. The best advice is to be alert for unusual reactions."

—Traveling Healthy

South America, Egypt, or some similar destination where *Salmonella* is common.

Danger Signals of Diarrhea

If your diarrhea is accompanied by any of the following, you should **consult a doctor.**

- severe abdominal pain
- high fever
- shaking chills
- blood in watery stool
- vomiting

This is particularly true if your symptoms have not improved within 12 or 24 hours after you started taking Imodium.

Constipation

The remedies you use to handle traveler's diarrhea might just send you over the edge the other direction. Drinking too little or not eating enough fiber-rich produce can cause sluggish bowels. Sitting long hours on airplanes compounds the problem. If you have constipation, increase your fluid intake and, if possible, get a little exercise. Also, eat fruit and other high-fiber foods, such as whole grain breads, potatoes, and vegetables. You should have packed a mild laxative in your travel kit. Read that section again if you need more information.

Allergies, Sinus Problems, and Asthma

If you suffer from hay fever, you can probably blame a runny nose and itchy eyes on plants that seasonally flood the air with microscopic pollens. Pollen seasons vary across the U.S. For example, in the Northeast and the Midwest, you will be affected from early March through mid-October.

In the Rockies and Great Plains the season of concern runs from mid-March through early September. In the Northwest and Northern California there are two seasons for pollens, early March to early June, and early August to mid-October. Central and Southern California has the longest and heaviest pollen season—from early January to early December. For the Southwest and the Southeast, the season runs February to November.

Mold spores also cause seasonal allergies. Mold thrives in warm, moist conditions, and spores abound after summer rains. They are present all year in the South but are rare in the nation's dry regions.

How to Handle Allergic Reactions When You're on the Road

Several effective over-the-counter medications are available for serious allergic reactions:

- Antihistamines relieve or prevent symptoms of allergic rhinitis by blocking histamine, the substance made by the body during an allergic reaction. Antihistamines can make you drowsy, however, so be cautious.

- Decongestants in tablets or nose-drop form relieve nasal and sinus congestion by narrowing blood vessels. Limit use of either type to a few a day, however, since increased congestion can occur when you stop. Oral decongestants may raise blood pressure so avoid them if you have high blood pressure.

- Bronchodilators are inhaled directly into the lungs to open the air passages and provide immediate relief from coughing, wheezing, and shortness of breath common to an asthma attack. You can use bronchodilators preventively before an allergy-triggering activity, although you should consult your doctor before using them.

You will want to consult with your doctor if you have chronic problems such as asthma, chronic sinusitis, or frequent allergy attacks. Prescription medications such as Seldane or Beconase nasal spray may be your best options if you have sinus problems regularly.

Allergies? Call (800) 765-5367 to hear a weekly forecast for pollen levels in the area you will be staying. Just punch in the zip code or state and city abbreviations.

Of course, if you are allergy prone you'll want to try to stay away from the substances that provoke an attack. Stay indoors if pollen counts are high; use pillows and blankets made of synthetic fibers; avoid foods to which

Allergic Reactions

you are allergic, and stay away from molds or moldy environments. Sometimes this is not possible when you travel, but if you think the shower curtain is moldy, be assertive and ask that it be changed or that you be moved to a less moldy room.

Another problem people with allergies face when they travel is the presence of sulfite, or other food additives, in restaurant foods. Sulfites should be avoided. Always ask if there are any sulfites in the food you plan to order, or if they are present in the wine or beer. And if you are asthmatic, it's a good idea to mention it to someone.

Exercise-Induced Allergic Reactions

People with asthma also need to be aware that heavy exercising can promote an attack. There are also people who, according to Dr. Thomas Welch, are "allergic" to exercise. Symptoms of itching, hives, wheezing, and abdominal cramping appear in some allergy-prone people after exercise. These symptoms are more likely to appear if you are allergic to certain pollens or dust. Although rare, taking some medications, especially aspirin, before running can bring on this type of reaction.

Preventing Exercise-Induced Allergic Reactions

1. Use an inhaled bronchodilator before your exercise.

2. Avoid eating for 2 hours or more before exercise.

As a precaution against a severe allergic reaction, you may want to have an adrenaline kit available, similar to that used for people who are allergic to bee stings. Also, if you are allergy prone or have asthma, always try to exercise with a friend, in the case that you do have trouble, you'll also have help.

If you have known allergies, asthma, or chronic sinusitis, take along your medicine, take your own allergy-free pillow, and have an extra supply of antihistamines (such as Benadryl or Actifed) on hand. Take precautions when you exercise.

Other ways to improve your health and minimize colds, allergies, sinusitis, and bronchitis include:

1. Request a smoke-free room.

2. Wash your hands often and keep them away from your face.

3. Rehydrate your body by drinking lots of water and by using an inexpensive baby room cold-water vaporizer as a humidifier.

Food and Water Safety

Most of us take the safety of our food and water for granted. Water purification and sanitation methods have resulted in freedom from infectious diseases transmitted by contaminated food and water for most of the United States and the Western world.

Despite the good safety record in North America, however, there are still 400 to 600 reported outbreaks of food- and water-borne illness reported each year in the U.S. Salmonellosis and hepatitis seem to be the most common. Gastroenteritis is occasionally reported from the Gulf Coast, and botulism, caused by improperly canned food, is sporadically reported nationwide.

Outside the U.S., Canada, Europe, Australia, and Japan, the incidence of food- and water-borne illness is much greater. Most developing countries do not have our standard of living, sanitation technology, or cultural bias toward the disposal of human fecal material.

In many tropical countries, diarrhea is the number one killer of infants and young children. If you are planning to travel to a country outside the Western world, you will want to consult *The International Travel Health Guide* by Dr. Stuart Rose, available from Travel Medicine, Inc. in Northampton, Massachusetts. Check your local library or call 1-800-872-8633 to order a copy.

The typical American inhales 81 pounds of debris every year.

"The average American eats out at restaurants 14,411 times in a lifetime, including 1,811 trips to McDonald's."

—In An Average Lifetime

Judging the Safety of a Restaurant

Choose restaurants carefully and get recommendations from the concierge. Some restaurants are cleaner than others, so if you are going someplace that you know nothing about, here's a quick checklist to help you decide if the restaurant is safe:

- Are the silverware, tables, glasses, and plates clean?
- Are the toilets clean? Are soap and hot water provided for hand washing?
- Are there flies? Flies carry disease germs.
- Is there adequate ventilation and a smoke-free section?
- Is there uncovered garbage outside?
- Are the servers well groomed?

Of course, a "no" answer to any of these questions means you should probably try another restaurant.

If you decide to eat food from street vendors, choose only food that is cooked, boiled, steamed, or grilled directly in front of you. Eat cold foods cold and hot foods hot. Avoid food that the vendor handles excessively after cooking. Avoid juices or other drinks unless they are commercially bottled and opened in your presence. And, eat only food that is served in a clean container.

If you buy fruit on the street, wash it, and buy only the kind that is completely covered with a fully removable peel, like oranges and bananas.

In most urban areas of the U.S., water is properly filtered and chlorinated and so should be safe. However, sometimes in areas of drought even the tap water can be tainted. You should never drink tap water in a developing country. If you suspect that the water is not totally pure, or if you have diarrhea of obscure origin, drink bottled water. You might even want to brush your teeth in bottled water. And if necessary, take along some Potable Aqua iodine tablets or chlorine to disinfect any water you plan to drink.

Specific Concerns

Some of the most common health concerns are headaches, back pain, "flu," colds, fevers, and sore throats. The following sections will help you decide when to treat these common illnesses on your own and when you need to call in a doctor.

Headaches

Air travel frequently causes headaches, says Alan M. Rapoport, M.D., director of the Stamford, Connecticut-based New England Center for Headaches. Altitude may lower your threshold to headaches. The atmospheric pressure in a jet aircraft cabin at a cruising altitude of 35,000 feet (10,500 meters) is roughly equivalent to being on a mountain at an altitude between 5,000 and 7,500 feet (1,500 and 2,000 meters). This can cause blood vessels in the head to dilate and cause pain.

The most common headaches aloft are tension-type headaches, which are due to excitement, stress, different eating and sleeping schedules, prolonged and uncomfortable sitting, and other factors inherent to air travel. Tension headaches involve moderate pressure on both sides of the head, and, sometimes, the top of the head, says Dr. Rapoport.

"Aspirin was first marketed in 1899 by the German company Farbenfabriken Bayer A.G. It quickly became the world's largest selling nonprescription drug—first available as a loose powder in individual doses in small envelopes, then as capsules. Tablets were introduced by Bayer in 1915."

—The Browser's Book of Beginnings

To minimize the headaches of traveling, get to the airport early, relax, and get an aisle seat so you can easily stretch and walk around. You should also watch the food you eat because it can cause migraine and cluster headaches. Migraine headaches are severe, throbbing, and often one-sided pains, and may be associated with nausea and sensitivity to light and sound. Cluster headaches are excruciating, steady, boring pains in and around one eye that may last 1 to 2 hours. They are associated with a red or teary eye and a stuffed and running nostril on the side of the pain.

If you suffer from migraine headaches, pre-order fruit platters or vegetarian dinners for flights. These meals generally do not contain MSG and other preservatives which may cause a migraine. Also avoid cold cuts, strong cheeses, and other items that contain nitrates. Other foods known to cause migraine headaches, include: pickled and preserved foods, chocolate, avocados, onions, pizza, citrus fruit, red wine, and artificial sweeteners in some carbonated beverages.

Most headaches can be relieved by over-the-counter preparations, (which are available from flight attendants), but for severe headaches, ask for ice and apply it to your temples or back of your neck.

Headache Triggers

Besides air travel and some foods, headaches can be caused by other specific triggers. According to Dr. Thomas Welch, these are:

1. Chewing gum—The relentless grinding tires the muscles around the jaw and may cause pain at the front and sides of the head.

2. Ice cream—Sudden cooling of the roof of the mouth causes two nerves and the tissues in that area to hurry pain signals to the brain.

3. Salt—Too much salt can bring on migraine headaches, often hours after eating it.

4. Sun—Too much sun dehydrates your body, depleting the fluids around the brain and spinal column. This causes the blood vessels to rub against these surrounding tissues and their nerves and can cause pain.

5. Overexertion—During strenuous exercise, small blood vessels may not be able to expand fast enough to accommodate the increased blood flow. Pressure from backed-up blood can build up in the arteries, stretching the walls and causing a headache.

6. High heels—Wearing high heels can tense back muscles. This tension can spread up into the head and neck, causing headaches.

Handling a Headache

Here's a quick relaxation exercise when you have a headache or feel a lot of tension in your facial muscles:

- Squeeze your eyes shut for 7 seconds
- Let your lids go limp
- Squeeze your eyes shut half as tightly as before
- Relax
- Squeeze again, half as tightly as the last time
- Relax
- Repeat, each time halving the muscle tension
- Repeat this halving exercise until your entire forehead is free of tension and stressful energy

From an interview of Keith Sedlacek, M.D., author of The Sedlacek Technique, as found in 201 Things to Do While You're Getting Better, CHRONIMED Publishing, Minneapolis: 1993.

Back Pain

Back pain can occur when you travel, especially if you carry a garment bag slung over your shoulder down lengthy airport corridors or have a stuffed briefcase or carry-on bag that stretches one of your arms longer than the other. Of course, your best defense against back pain is being physically fit.

Poor posture, improper lifting habits, prolonged standing, a stressful trip, and declining physical fitness can all add up to back pain.

To protect yourself from pain, practice good posture, exercise to stay physically fit, and be aware that the luggage you're schlepping can be hazardous to your health. Get a cart or hire a red cap to help you get to the gate or to a taxi. Don't stuff one bag under your arm, throw another over your shoulder, and drag a third behind you. This unnatural distribution of weight causes stress on your back and your spine. If you must carry your own luggage, find a way to balance the load by distributing it evenly in both arms.

Back Pain

Dr. Daniel Kurtti, a rehabilitation specialist, suggests that during an episode of temporary back pain, the following steps are safe and effective self-care solutions:

1. Take aspirin. While no drug can speed up the healing process, aspirin should provide relief from occasional pain. If you are aspirin-sensitive, acetaminophen (as found in Tylenol) is a good choice, as is ibuprofen, which is a little stronger and found in Advil.

2. Use ice packs on the sore area to keep any inflammation down. Bed rest can be helpful, but if lying down is uncomfortable, put a pillow under your knees.

3. After the first few days, during which you should have been using ice packs, switch to warm packs to increase blood circulation and healing. Light massages or warm baths may also help provide relief. Only after a few days of treatment with cold packs should you enter a hot tub or jacuzzi.

4. Carefully reintroduce physical activity after the attack. Gradual stretches and regular walking are good ways to get back into action.

5. Learn some safe back exercises. Modified sit-ups and low-back stretches are recommended.

6. Take the time to relax. Tension will only make your backache worse.

Fever

Your body's temperature is an important barometer of how well you are dealing with germs. For good health, the body works best at a temperature of about 97 to 99 degrees Fahrenheit.

By itself, a high temperature is not necessarily cause for concern—it can actually be a perfectly normal way for your body to defend itself against infection. Your body shivers to help produce the heat it needs to fight germs and sweats to regulate the rise in temperature.

If you are elderly or have a history of heart or lung disease or other chronic conditions, then a fever is a special cause for concern. But for most people, there is no medical reason to try to reduce a fever unless it is accompanied by other symptoms of illness. Use common sense and save some energy to heal yourself.

Self-Care Steps for Handling a Fever

1. With no other symptoms, medication is not necessary. But if the fever makes you uncomfortable, take aspirin or acetaminophen (as found in Tylenol).

2. Increase the amount of fluids you drink to a minimum of eight glasses a day. When you have a fever, you lose bodily fluids, so it's important to prevent dehydration.

3. It may help to cool your body by sponging or taking a bath in cool water (70-75°). However, you should seek medical attention if you have a temperature greater than 101.6° along with any of the following:

- earache, persistent sore throat, productive cough
- pain in the lower abdomen
- back pain or painful urination
- persistent headache and stiff neck
- frequent vomiting

And if you have a fever over 101.6° with no other symptoms but lasting longer than 2 days, call a doctor.

The Common Cold

A cold is uncomfortable—it's tough to just grin and bear it, but it is usually just an inconvenience. There are no confirmed strategies for preventing colds; taking large doses of vitamin C has not proven effective. Still, there are a variety of measures you can take to reduce your chances of catching a cold and to minimize your symptoms as you wait for a cold to pass.

- Wash your hands often, and avoid hand contact with people who have colds.

The Common Cold

- Raise the humidity in the hotel by placing bowls or buckets of water near the radiators. Or, purchase a low-cost, cool-air vaporizer at a local pharmacy and run it near your bed.
- Remain up and about whenever possible. You may benefit from extra rest, but generally, you'll feel better by staying moderately active.
- Drink extra fluids during the day.
- If you develop a sore throat, gargle with slightly salted, hot water.

When it comes to colds, a physician's advice is not much better than your mother's. No matter how much money you spend on drug-store remedies, you can't do better than aspirin or chicken soup.

Sometimes cold symptoms may actually be signs of a more serious illnesses. Call a doctor if you have:

- An oral temperature over 101.6° lasting longer than 48 hours.
- Persistent coughing lasting longer than 3 to 5 days, or cough that produces thick green, yellow, or grey phlegm.

Sore Throat

A sore throat can be annoying, but it usually does not represent a serious health threat. Low humidity, failing to drink enough fluids, winter dryness, or smoke can cause sore throats.

Two types of infections cause sore throats: the more common viral infection, and the less common—but more serious—bacterial infection, known as strep throat. Even doctors cannot distinguish between viral and bacterial sore throats without a throat culture, but here are the usual differences between the two:

Common Sore Throat

- Is caused by a virus;
- Is less likely to be accompanied by a fever;
- Is sometimes associated with cold or flu.

Strep Throat

- Is caused by bacteria;
- Causes the throat to appear very red with white patches or pus and swollen glands;
- Often produces a temperature of 101.6°;
- Requires treatment with an antibiotic.

The more common type of sore throat will go away in a few days—although even 7 to 10 days is not uncommon. But with strep throat, you need to be careful. If left untreated, strep can lead to heart problems (known as rheumatic fever).

Coping With a Sore Throat

If your sore throat is the common variety associated with cold or flu, you have little cause for concern. Avoid environmental irritants such as smoke, smog, chalk, dust, and allergens. Also, avoid the dehydrating effects of alcohol or caffeine from coffee, tea, or soft drinks. You can also try these measures:

- Drink fluids. Up to eight glasses a day will soothe your throat and loosen mucus for a more productive cough.

- Gargle with warm saltwater. Add about a teaspoon of salt to a glass of water. Most mouthwashes have no medicinal value for preventing or relieving a sore throat and are no more effective than saltwater.

- Suck on hard candies or cough drops and take aspirin for fever or discomfort.

- Increase the humidity with vaporizers or hot showers.

Earaches

There are many possible causes for earaches—the most common being an infection of the middle ear. These can result from a build-up of fluid in the middle ear and the eustachian tube, a small channel that drains fluid from the ear into the nose. When this tube becomes clogged, it can become a breeding ground for bacteria. Once the fluid is infected with bacteria, you've got a middle ear infection, and that requires treatment with an antibiotic.

Earaches can occur with colds. To reduce the risk of worsening your earache and to relieve the pain:

1. Take an antibiotic. These are only available by prescription, but if you have discussed your travels with your doctor, you may have some in your travel kit. Take these per your doctor's instructions. It is very important to continue taking the antibiotics even after the pain of the earache is gone.

2. If your earache persists, see a doctor, and continue to see the doctor per his or her recommendations to prevent complications or future ear problems.

3. For relief from pain and to help you sleep, use acetaminophen (as in Tylenol) instead of aspirin. Ear drops may also provide temporary relief.

4. Since earaches are commonly associated with colds, drink plenty of fluids.

"Swimmer's Ear"

Swimmer's ear is an infection of the outer part of the ear canal and usually results from water in the ear. It is associated with an itchy feeling, redness of the outer ear, and pain from simply wiggling the ear. While ear wax is a normal, protective secretion, it can sometimes become impacted and difficult to remove.

For ear problems, try these steps:

1. To prevent swimmer's ear, dry your ears after a swim with a clean towel or hair dryer. You may also want to use drying ear drops as recommended by your doctor.

2. If ear wax has built up, do not probe in the ear with swabs. Instead, direct a hot shower into your ear to loosen the wax. Then wipe it out with a clean towel. Don't try to wash your ear if you think you have ruptured your ear drum or if you have ear drainage. A heating pad or warm cloth may also provide relief.

3. Simple ear stuffiness is often quickly relieved by closing your mouth, plugging your nose, and gently forcing air into your blocked nasal passages, similar to the technique suggested for use during airplane descent. Chewing gum may also relieve the pressure.

4. If you have had experience with your earache before, use Vōsol according to your doctor's directions. If your ear stuffiness or blocked ear passages do not respond to any of these steps, see a doctor.

Sunburn

You can get a nasty sunburn, even in winter, if you are cruising in tropical water or skiing at high altitudes. If your business travel requires you to hit a hot spot in the summer, there are some things you'll want to know.

To protect yourself, wear a hat and cover yourself with lightweight loose clothing. Wear a sunscreen with a sun protective factor (SPF) of at least 15 on all exposed skin. The 15 means you can stay in the sun 15 minutes longer than it would usually take for your skin to burn, so be cautious even when you use a sunscreen. There is little evidence that an SPF rating of 30 is much more effective, but if you have experience with one that works for you, that's the one to choose. Avoid the midday sun. If you must be in the sun, put your sunscreen on at least 30 minutes before you venture out.

Swimming Dangers

Fresh and salt water can carry parasites that are hazardous to swimmers. Beaches all over the world are polluted. If you plan to swim, check with local authorities to find out which beaches are safest. Just because there are lots of people swimming in the area doesn't mean that the water is pollution-free. You may not have the same tolerance for water-borne bacteria as the local population.

Swimming Dangers

Drowning is another danger of swimming in unfamiliar waters. Next to auto accidents, swimming poses the greatest danger to your health as a traveler. Never swim at an unprotected beach, and never swim alone, anywhere. If you find a beach that looks appealing but is totally deserted, it's best to move on to one where there are some people.

Also, sea urchins, Man of War jelly fish, and spiny crabs or lobsters can cause you harm. If you should step on a sea urchin, do not attempt to pull the spine out of your foot yourself. The barbs can break off and cause infection. Ask a lifeguard to help you or have the guard call a paramedic if you need one. Poisonous jellyfish cause some uncomfortable stinging sensations, but they are usually not fatal. Always be prepared, though. Check out the dangers of the area before you go to the beach or into the water.

Air Pollution

Dirty air is likewise hazardous to your health, particularly if you are elderly or have heart or respiratory problems. Mexico City tops the list of places with foul air. Other smoggy spots include Cairo, Beijing, London, Seoul, and Los Angeles. If your business takes you to one of these places, you'll want to go easy on the outdoor exercise.

Nosebleeds

The most frequent cause of nosebleeds is dryness. People who travel long hours in dry airplanes and then move from one dry, overheated hotel room to another are liable to experience nasal hemorrhage or common nosebleed.

Step one in preventing nosebleeds is to neutralize the effects of a dry environment. On a long flight, drink lots of water. Also, any hotel or motel room can be overly dry if it is too warm. People with a history of nosebleeds should have a vaporizer or moisturizer. Placing a pan of water on a radiator and allowing the water to evaporate into the room also works. If none of these are available, run a hot shower and let the steam out from the bathroom into the sleeping area of your room. Also, put a small amount of lubricating jelly into each nostril at night, especially if you've had nosebleeds before.

Normally the body is good at regulating its temperature. But the mechanisms responsible for maintaining a steady 98.6° can break down in the following circumstances:

Heat Problems

1. When the temperature outside the body is greater than that of the blood being carried to the skin surface. Since heat is no longer lost by radiation in these conditions, one of the three cooling mechanisms is lost. In addition, if the sun is shining, the body absorbs heat instead of loses it.

2. When the humidity is also increased, the ability to sweat is impaired. If in this setting you don't drink enough fluids, this can cause serious trouble. The body doesn't have the wherewithal to sweat so the amount of heat it can lose via the skin is drastically reduced. It's important to avoid dehydration.

3. If you're overdressed, of course, the heat will affect you more quickly.

4. In some older travelers, the temperature-regulating mechanism, like other bodily functions, has become slightly less efficient. Challenged by excessive heat, the signals that initiate the sweating, the blood shunting, and the fluid shifting are delayed or inadequate.

5. Some medications increase your susceptibility to heat:

—Phenothiazines (like Thorazine or Compazine) that interfere with the brain's ability to regulate body heat;

—Drugs that reduce your ability to sweat (this list is long, and includes antihistamines, certain medications for Parkinson's disease, several antispasmodics taken for intestinal irritability, and other psychiatric drugs);

—Drugs that increase heat production like amphetamines and cocaine;

—Diuretics, which remove body water (during a heat wave, that's precisely what you don't want to happen).

The secret to preventing heat problems is simply drinking enough water both before and during exercise. There are other fluids on the market, but water seems to be the best.

—Minute Health Tips

Remember, alcohol increases the body's heat production and so should also be avoided in hot weather. Certain diseases like diabetes and heart trouble may interfere with the body's ability to lose heat. For instance, some people with diabetes may have difficulty sweating (technically it is called autonomic neuropathy). Finally, when the heart is weak and can't pump the blood adequately, less of it gets to the skin, where heat is dissipated.

Heatstroke

The most serious form of heat injury is heatstroke. This usually occurs in the setting of very high outdoor temperatures (greater than 95°F.) and high humidity, especially in bright sun. Heatstroke is often sudden, and results from the total breakdown of the body's heat-regulating mechanisms. At first, the individual stops sweating, then confusion sets in, followed by coma and seizures. Body temperature shoots up to 106°F. This condition is a serious medical emergency and requires hospitalization. If you are thinking of going out walking or touring on a very hot day in a very humid climate, do it with a companion.

Heat Exhaustion

Heat exhaustion is another severe consequence of excessive exposure to heat. The symptoms include: nausea, vomiting, muscle cramps, fainting, and a rapid, weak pulse. Prevention involves keeping cool, applying cold compresses, and drinking plenty of fluids. Extra salt is not necessary and should be avoided, especially by those with high blood pressure or heart trouble.

Heat Cramps

Another heat-related illness is the occurrence of heat cramps. These are painful spasms that athletes experience in the muscles they use most. During hot weather, cut back on your exercise, particularly if you exercise outdoors. Give your body a few extra days to get acclimatized. If you are going to exercise out of doors in a warm climate, do so early in the morning or late in the afternoon or early evening before it gets too hot or after the sun has set.

In a recent study, the leading cause of death to U.S. travelers in Mexico was injuries, most from motor vehicle crashes. Many road accidents involving tourists don't involve a collision between two vehicles, instead they are usually due to a loss of driver control resulting from fatigue, alcohol, or driving in unfamiliar or difficult road conditions.

To Prevent Automobile Accidents

Auto Safety

1. Always drive with caution, especially where roads are not well marked.

Use particular caution in those countries where they drive on the left side of the road. Certain cities around the world are notorious for traffic dangers. If you are planning to drive in Rome, Paris, or London, be sure to learn where you're going well ahead of time. In the U.S., you can contact the American Automobile Association to get directions and help.

2. Don't drink and drive. Drive only when you are in good physical condition, not when you are tired or hung over.

3. Where the traffic circle is used at intersections, the approaching driver must yield the right of way to those already in the circle. Once you are in the circle you supposedly have the right of way, but be careful not to cut off anyone who is exiting.

4. Try not to drive at night. Not all roads are well marked or lighted. Also, emergency help is less available at night.

5. Consider hiring a qualified guide or driver.

6. Rent a large, not a small, vehicle.

7. Always wear your seat belt.

8. Be sure you are covered by collision and liability insurance.

"Recent studies of truck drivers show that the accident rate doubles when drivers have been on the road for more than eight hours."

—The Diabetic Traveler

Even though we hear and read about political kidnappings, acts of terrorism, and plane hijackings, you should probably be more concerned about losing your luggage, drowning, falling, and overuse of alcohol or drugs.

General Safety Measures

These guidelines will help ensure your travel safety:

1. Avoid small, nonscheduled airlines, especially abroad.

2. Review hotel fire safety rules and locate the exits nearest your room.

3. If possible, get a room between the second and seventh floors—high enough to prevent easy entrance by an intruder and low enough for fire equipment to reach.

4. Lock your hotel room at all times.

5. If you are drinking alcohol, don't relax by sitting on the railing of your hotel balcony. Falls and serious injuries often occur just this way.

6. Don't travel at night outside of urban areas. Even then, don't drive at night.

7. Never pick up hitchhikers.

8. If you go out at night, stay in a group.

9. Don't go out to beaches at night.

Of Special Interest

Diabetes

Dr. Joseph Juliano suggests that people with diabetes carry a diabetes identification card at all times. This lists your name, address, phone number, physician, and emergency symptoms for people unfamiliar with diabetes. Identification bracelets and neck chains are also available. For more information before you go, contact the American Diabetes Association, or ask your doctor for more specific travel tips that relate to your specific situation.

Consult *The Diabetic Traveler,* a six-page quarterly newsletter for people with diabetes. Subscription information is found on page 172. The newsletter also offers a wallet-sized insulin adjustment guide for travel through time zones.

If you are traveling outside the U.S. and need to clear Customs both coming and going, carry a letter from your doctor substantiating that you have diabetes.

Be even more careful managing your diet when you travel. If you think you'll be in an airplane for longer than your body can handle without proper food, take some with you. If you need special meals, order them ahead of time. An orange or an apple, some crackers with peanut butter, or a half-pint of orange juice should be included in your carry-on bag. Always be prepared for unexpected delays when you travel and pay close attention to the timing of your meals and snacks.

If you're traveling from one time zone to another, you'll want to ask your doctor for some special guidance in making the proper adjustment in insulin injections. Also, taking an in-flight injection will require less air due to cabin pressure.

If you are carrying fruit and you're traveling into some states in the U.S. and most foreign countries of Europe, know that agricultural restrictions apply. You cannot take a Florida orange to California, nor can you enter most European countries with fresh fruit on your person or in your luggage.

Diabetes and Safe Travel

The Diabetic Traveler offers these additional travel tips:

1. Test your blood glucose more frequently than usual.

2. Pack extra syringes, insulin, and other diabetic supplies (twice as much as you think you'll need) and divide them into at least two separate containers. Always keep the supplies with you, since any baggage you don't carry is inaccessible and could be misplaced.

Diabetes and Safe Travel

3. Be careful of temperature extremes (for example, the baggage compartment of an airplane) that will damage insulin.

4. Protect your insulin and supplies in appropriate cases.

5. Bring two half-finished bottles of insulin rather than one full one, even if there is more than enough for the duration of the trip. Accidental breakage or loss won't leave you without necessary supplies.

6. Pack glucagon, which is administered intravenously in cases of extreme hypoglycemia (low blood sugar). Glucagon is available by prescription.

Arthritis

If arthritis complicates your travel life, be sure to manage it effectively when you're on the road. If you must travel during a flare up, get plenty of rest. Take your medications as your doctor has prescribed them, and be assertive about asking for any extra assistance you may need.

If you're attending a business conference, book a room in the same hotel, if possible, to avoid commuting. It's even better if the hotel has heated pools for exercise and relaxation. And request a room that is equipped with the tools you need: handrails in the bathroom and shower, the firmness of mattress you need on the bed, and extra pillows to help comfort your areas of pain. A lack of good quality sleep can significantly contribute to the feeling of fatigue that accompanies many forms of arthritis.

Sleeping away from home can sometimes be less than restful. You may find yourself sleeping for 10 hours, but you don't feel rested in the morning. Any cause of sleep disturbance—waking at night from pain or even getting up frequently to go to the bathroom—may mean you will awaken more tired than refreshed. If this happens, you may want to contact a doctor to obtain a sleeping aid. If you have experienced this during travel before, talk to your doctor before you go and include a sleeping aid as part of your travel kit.

The most important management tool if you have arthritis is to pace yourself. Take things at a pace that you can handle and remember that your health is more important than your job. For more information on travel and arthritis, write the Arthritis Foundation, P.O. Box 19000, Atlanta, GA 30326, or call your local chapter.

Infectious Diseases

Relatively few foreign trips call for immunization anymore, but for those that do, you must act well ahead of your departure. Certain shots must be given long before landing on foreign soil. See your doctor 4 to 6 weeks before you take off for the tropics. And don't overlook routine inoculations such as tetanus or flu shots.

The World Health Organization publishes periodic bulletins about areas where infectious diseases are active. The Centers for Disease Control and Prevention offers a 24-hour hotline (404) 332-4559 with updated recorded messages about requirements and recommendations for international travel.

The U.S. State Department keeps a listing of countries where the traveler may be at risk. They can be contacted by calling (202) 647-5225. Multipage advisories are also available from the *World Status Map* at (800) 322-4685 and International Alert at (800) 336-8334.

There are also scores of travel health clinics in the U.S. that are staffed by doctors specializing in travel medicine. For a directory of clinics, send a self-addressed stamped (98 cents postage) 9- by 11-inch envelope to Dr. Leonard Marcus, Traveler's Health and Immunization Services, 148 Highland Ave., Newton, MA 02165.

Malaria

In recent years, drug-resistant malaria has emerged in many parts of the world. Chloroquine, long used to prevent malaria, has become nearly useless against this new strain. A new drug, Lariam (generically known as mefloquine), is effective, but it's losing strength in Southeast Asia and parts of Africa. Doxycycline can combat strains that have outwitted other drugs, but should not be given to pregnant women or children.

Check with your doctor before you travel to the tropics to see if you need antimalarial medication. You can also call the 24-hour malaria hotline run by the Centers of Disease Control at (404) 332-4555. Also, wherever malaria is a problem, ward off mosquitoes with an insect repellent containing 20 to 30 percent DEET. The best bet is to avoid exposure to mosquitoes in areas where malaria is known to be active.

Sexually Transmitted Diseases

Among the most insidious dangers facing today's traveler is the risk of AIDS or other sexually transmitted diseases.

The Centers for Disease Control has issued this advisory:

Acquired Immunodeficiency Syndrome (AIDS) is a consequence of infection by the human immunodeficiency virus (HIV). Other less severe illnesses, sometimes grouped under the term AIDS-related complex (ARC), as well as asymptomatic infection may also result from infection with HIV. The incubation period for AIDS may be long, ranging from a few months to several years. Some individuals infected with HIV remain asymptomatic for 5 years or more. Currently, there is no vaccine to protect against infection with HIV, and there is no cure for AIDS.

Travelers are at increased risk if they: have sexual intercourse (homosexual or heterosexual) with an infected person; use or allow the use of contaminated unsterilized syringes or needles for any injections, e.g., illicit drugs, tattooing, acupuncture, or medical/dental procedures; or use infected blood, blood components, or clotting factor concentrates. This would be an extremely rare occurrence in those countries or cities where donated blood/plasma is screened for HIV antibody.

Travelers should avoid sexual encounters with a person who is thought to be infected with HIV or whose HIV infection status is unknown. This will mean avoiding sexual activity with intravenous drug users and persons with multiple sexual partners, including male or female prostitutes. Condoms may reduce, but not entirely eliminate, transmission of HIV. Persons who engage in vaginal, anal, or oral-genital intercourse with anyone who is infected with HIV or whose infection status is unknown should use condoms. Diaphragms in combination with a spermicide may give additional protection.

Sexual contact is the major route of spreading HIV worldwide. That means the prevention of AIDS is largely under your control. If you choose to be sexually active, choosing a low-risk partner is critically important. If traveling, you may not have enough time to know the other person well enough to know your level of risk. The following list may help you identify high-risk partners:

Individuals more apt to be HIV positive include:

- Homosexual or bisexual men
- Drug addicts
- Prostitutes
- Hemophiliacs
- Recipients of multiple blood transfusions
- People with venereal disease

You should avoid high-risk individuals for many reasons: (1) You don't want VD; (2) They may have had many sexual partners; (3) They are more likely to carry the AIDS virus; (4) If they have active venereal disease and genital ulcers, they can more easily transmit the AIDS virus. Also, if you have a venereal disease like herpes, syphilis, chancroid, or gonorrhea, you are more susceptible to getting AIDS from a partner infected with HIV.

AIDS is not spread through:

- Casual contact
- Touching or hugging
- Handshaking
- Coughing or sneezing
- Insect or mosquito bites
- Food or water
- Eating utensils, cups, or plates
- Toilets
- Swimming pools or baths

"AIDS is now the sixth leading cause of death in American women aged 15 to 44."

—FDA Consumer

For general information on AIDS, call the Centers for Disease Control National AIDS Hotline at (800) 342-AIDS.

You can avoid contracting AIDS if you:

- Abstain from sex.
- Have sex only with a monogamous, noninfected partner.
- Avoid contaminated blood, syringes, and needles.

If you are otherwise sexually active, you should:

- Avoid sex with high-risk partners.
- Always use a condom.

In addition to AIDS, you can acquire other sexually transmitted diseases caused by a variety of agents:

1. Virus-caused: AIDS, Hepatitis B, Hepatitis C, Hepatitis A (from oral-anal contact), genital herpes, and genital warts.

2. Bacteria-caused: Gonorrhea, syphilis, chancroid, chlamydia infections.

3. Protozoa-caused: Trichomonas infections.

Hepatitis

Although not as lethal, hepatitis B is more infectious than AIDS and is more easily spread by person-to-person contact. Hepatitis B is on the increase all over the world, including the U.S. In unvaccinated people, hepatitis B occurs from 40 to 180 days after exposure. The most common response is an asymptomatic infection.

Your illness may last several weeks to several months, but you have a 90 to 95 percent chance of recovering completely and having lifelong immunity against further attacks. A very small percentage of people, however, never get rid of the virus and become carriers who can infect others. Carriers are also at risk to develop chronic hepatitis, cirrhosis, and liver cancer. You should, therefore, take every precaution against the virus.

Your risk of getting hepatitis B can be reduced or eliminated by practicing safe sex, avoiding drugs, and being vaccinated. Immunization will protect you against hepatitis B. There are two types of vaccines available, those derived from human plasma, and those that are genetically engineered from yeast. Both are completely safe and virtually 100 percent effective after three doses.

Areas where up to 10 percent of the population are carriers of the hepatitis B virus are considered high-risk countries. If your travels take you to sub-Saharan-Africa; Southeast Asia, which includes China, Korea, and Indonesia; the South Pacific islands; the interior Amazon Basin; or Haiti and the Dominican Republic, you must protect yourself against this virus.

Travelers to the above areas are at risk if they are exposed to the blood or body fluids of infected people. Circumstances in which disease transmission occurs include receiving unscreened blood transfusions, unsafe injections from unclean needles or syringes, sexual contact, or close contact with carriers of the virus who have open sores on their skin caused by tropical ulcers, impetigo, scabies, or infected insect bites.

Other forms of hepatitis (A, C, and E) are also on the rise. Symptoms can be variable, but the classics include fatigue, loss of appetite, jaundice, dark urine, fever, abdominal pain, and aching joints. A blood test confirms the diagnosis.

Hepatitis A is likely to occur where food and water is contaminated. Shellfish are often suspect if eaten from areas where sanitation is poor.

For a list of English-speaking doctors in other countries, before your trip call the International Association for Medical Assistance to Travelers at (716) 754-4883.

Hepatitis C has been associated with blood transfusions, so be very cautious if you require blood transfusions in lesser-developed countries.

Hepatitis E is usually transmitted by drinking sewage-contaminated water. You must seek out professional medical treatment for any form of hepatitis.

5

ESPECIALLY FOR WOMEN

Protecting Yourself

As much as we hate to deal with it, crime is rampant across the world. Terrorism continues to threaten many international travelers, and recently it arrived in New York, threatening visitors and residents alike in the World Trade Center bombing.

Among the other annoyances you may confront on the road as a woman traveler are the possibility of injury from attack, harassment from male counterparts, discrimination from hotel and restaurant staff, and extra fatigue that relates to gender-biased imbalance of work assignments.

Terrorism is one of the most dangerous threats to any traveler. Information on how to deal with terrorism is found in the next chapter.

Women who are asked to travel to certain urban areas will want to exercise caution against personal attack if they must walk any distances in unsafe areas, return to the hotel alone after dark, or conduct their business in a less-than-secure environment.

There are a number of ways to protect yourself. Of course, the best of these is to avoid any of the perilous scenarios just listed. If you must put yourself at risk, however, you'll want to know something about self-defense.

There are a number of techniques that are part of the martial arts repertoire of self-defense. Karate has been found to be very effective and is quite suitable for women. The movements of this martial art are excellent for maintaining your agility.

Keep a low profile when traveling alone. Try not to advertise that you're alone, and register with only your first initial and last name.

The latest safety concern is criminals posing as hotel and motel staff. A guest gets a call from the 'front desk' and is told someone will be up shortly to make a repair. However, when the knock comes and the door is opened, it's a criminal. If you get a call from the front desk, call back to check it out.

The psychology of this self-defense form also tends to increase your sense of power, and empowerment is one of the keys to protecting yourself. Using a loud voice to intone threatening sounds is another part of karate that helps to increase a sense of menace against an enemy.

If you would like to learn some karate for self-defense, there is a national association that accredits teachers and trainers in the U.S. You'll want to check out a training source and be sure its accredited before you enroll.

Also, when you find a karate studio, ask for names of other students to call and get their impressions and recommendations.

A second and very serious way to protect yourself if you must go into situations where you're at risk is to become licensed and carry a handgun. We do not recommend this, but it is an alternative.

You'll want to talk this over with local police authorities and get recommendations about what would be the appropriate weapon for you. Also, you'll want to be thoroughly trained in handgun safety long before you'll ever be in need of one.

Do not purchase a gun from any source other than a reputable and established dealer. Get help from your local police department to find out where to go to purchase a legal handgun.

If your travel takes you to other states or overseas, you'll want to be sure you know and understand the regulations over personal weapons before you go.

There are alternatives to the handgun for self protection. Mace has long been used, but there are newer defensive chemical tools that temporarily disable an attacker, whether human or animal.

Again you should contact your local authorities to find out what is legal in your area before you purchase anything.

The U.S. Postal Service uses a chemical agent to protect mail carriers from animal attacks. This chemical temporarily blinds and stuns the animal without lasting effect. This is a much more benign protection method than possibly killing an assailant with a handgun and it is probably more effective.

Besides avoiding situations where you will be at risk, the current school of thought about how best to protect yourself suggests that you become as passive as possible.

If you are being robbed, it is best to turn over your money rather than risk death or permanent injury from some lunatic with a gun. It is a good idea to carry around $250 on your person so that if you are robbed, the criminal will be satisfied with the cash and will leave you alone. You can always get money, but your life and safety are not so easy to replace.

Always check with hotel management about local crime conditions in your destination. Be sure you know what areas are safe, especially if you want to go out after dark.

Calling the local police authorities for advice is a good idea if you must drive around a strange city. They can route you through areas that put you at less risk. If you really need to conduct your business in perilous situations, you may want to consider hiring an off-duty police escort who can act as a bodyguard.

Finally, learn to scream. Screaming usually disarms an attacker in the same way a burglar alarm protects a home. The noise attracts attention to the situation and can sometimes scare the criminal away. If the attacker has a gun, and if you assess the situation to be one of extreme danger, use your best judgment to placate and humor the criminal to save yourself from personal injury.

Safety Tips

1. Dress conservatively when you travel.
2. Don't display your airline tickets or cash.
3. Don't tote expensive luggage. It marks you as an easy target.

Vulnerable target areas of an attacker:

1. Eyes—Temporarily blind your attacker by striking or poking one or both eyes.
2. Throat—Press or hit the Adam's apple.
3. Groin—Strike upward between the legs with foot, knee, or fist.

Avoid staying in a hotel or motel with rooms that open to the outside— to a parking lot, courtyard, or other area with easy public access.

4. Be conservative about how much and what kind of jewelry you wear.
5. Always lock your hotel room.
6. Use the hotel safe deposit boxes to store valuables.
7. Ask for hotel rooms between the 3rd and 10th floors.
8. Do not display your hotel key.
9. Be very careful to keep company confidential information in a safe place. Industrial espionage is widespread.
10. If you carry a handbag, carry one with a short shoulder strap so that the purse itself is tightly under your armpit when you walk.
11. Be selective about who you talk to and be cautious about telling strangers where you are staying.
12. Keep in close touch with your family or friends at home and tell them to expect your calls at regularly scheduled intervals.
13. If you drive, never stop by the roadside to sleep.
14. Never pick up hitchhikers.
15. Don't hang out in bars.

Here's a relaxation technique that can help you when you are feeling frightened or are trying to recover from a scare:

Bring your awareness into the present by listening to the sounds around you, both inside and outside your hotel room. Let them come and go.

Bring your attention to the top of your head and imagine a wave of relaxation beginning to flow through that area of your body, melting away all tension. Allow that wave to flow downwards through each part of your body, jaw, neck, shoulders, etc. Use your attention to systematically go through your body, from head to foot, until every part is relaxed. If you like, you can use the idea of breathing relaxation in through the top of your head and breathing tension out through the bottoms of your feet.

When you have been through your whole body, take a couple of deep breaths. As you breathe out, allow yourself to feel more and more deeply relaxed. You can either rest in this state for a while or go on to include the next steps.

Imagine yourself in a beautiful, natural place; it may be a place you know or a completely imaginary place. Absorb the peace and beauty of this place. Really note the details of what is around you. What is the ground like beneath your feet? What does the air feel like against your skin in this place, etc.

Imagine that there are some balloons nearby and that one by one you can tie each of your problems and fears to a balloon and watch it float away.

As you watch the last balloon float off, feel the golden warmth of the sun on your head and shoulders. Allow its golden radiance to warm and soothe your whole body, particularly any tense or painful areas.

Gradually bring yourself back. Become aware of your body and the room, and in your own time, open your eyes."

From Coping with Cancer: Making Sense of It All. By Rachael Clyne, Thorsons Publishing Group/Harper Collins Publishing; Wellingborough, England and New York: 1989.

Assertiveness Skills

While some women like to think sexual harassment is a dead issue, in the real world it is far from it. You may be the victim of insidious harassment almost anywhere.

It will probably take another generation before men learn to deal with women truly as equals in the business environment. If you are confronted with offensive behaviors from your male counterparts, blow the whistle on them. Call that behavior to their attention in an assertive, not aggressive manner.

"Women comprise 26 percent of salespeople, up from 7 percent a decade ago."

—American Demographics

It is best not to use threats, but to state your position clearly and firmly. You might say:

"Hey, fellas, I like a good joke as well as the next person, but that was really over the line."

or

A recent poll of executives found that 90 percent pinpoint a negative attitude as a major reason employees are fired.

"I know you are a person of good taste and breeding, and that joke (or behavior) really doesn't become you."

or

"That kind of behavior (or joke) really makes you unattractive, and you're usually such a good-looking guy."

Use your imagination to develop your own retorts. Nothing will change if you simply ignore a chauvinistic attack. You don't have to alienate your coworkers or associates, nor do you have to become confrontational.

Learning to be assertive is to acquire a skill that will benefit you in all aspects of your life. Learning to state your position in a nonemotional way enables the situation to take on its own tone, freeing you up to be responsible only for your own role, and not for the outcome or the satisfaction of anyone else participating.

Be assertive in a friendly manner by using phrases like:

"I'd really appreciate it if you would..."

"I think we'd have a better outcome if..."

"You've always done such a nice job in the past, maybe you'd consider..."

"I need...so if you could just bear with me a moment..."

Using politeness and friendliness defuses any potentially confrontational situation making it possible to "have your cake and eat it, too."

There are often classes taught in assertiveness skills. If you think you need special training in this area, you'll want to take one.

Handling Discrimination

One of the more minor annoyances women confront is the discrimination they suffer from hotel or restaurant staffs. If two people get to the front desk at once and the clerk sees a man and a woman standing there, the clerk will usually speak to the man first. If this annoys you and you choose to do something about it, be assertive and say, "Excuse me, I think I was here first. And I'd like to check in."

Usually the clerk will immediately help you and the man will politely stand aside. If you choose to ignore this situation, and then you feel angry about it later, you'll want to do some personal work in stress management and assertiveness training.

If you're having dinner with a group of colleagues and the bill comes and is automatically given to one of the men at the table, speak up and say, "I'll take that," if you are responsible for the bill. If you're not responsible for it, say, "Thank you."

You do not have to sacrifice one bit of your femininity to be assertive. Practicing these skills will make you feel wonderful about yourself and you'll enjoy more of your activities. One word of caution: Don't look for discrimination where it doesn't really exist. Be certain of your perceptions. Don't mistake politeness and concern for something insulting or condescending.

Recognizing Your Limits

Sometimes for women who travel on business, there is a tendency on the part of management to assign more responsibilities for paper or clerical work to the female on the road over her male counterparts. Oftentimes you don't have a choice while you're away. But when you return to the office, you'll want to be sure and let management know that you are aware of the imbalance. Use your assertiveness skills to state your position clearly.

Beyond your work load, it's good to know your limits when you travel.

When you check in at a hotel, have the desk clerk write down your room number rather than saying it out loud for others to hear.

"When voicing a complaint for which you expect an adjustment, ask the person you're dealing with if he or she has the authority to make the adjustment. If not, ask to speak to someone who does."

—Sales & Marketing Management

If your schedule requires you to get up at 5:30 in the morning to get to the assignment by 7:30, obviously, you shouldn't stay up until 2 a.m. dancing the night away.

If you're scheduled for a meeting at 9 a.m., followed by a luncheon at 11:30 a.m., with another meeting at 1 p.m. and yet another at 3 p.m., followed by dinner at 6 p.m. and a debriefing at 9 p.m., you might be heading for burnout, particularly if this schedule is repeated the next day.

The stress of simply remembering the outcome of each of these meetings will cause you extra fatigue.

If you must participate in nonstop activities, be prepared. Carry a tape recorder and tape your notes. Use the machine to remind yourself of important personal care information, like "Don't forget to drink enough water today." Or "Remember to call home tonight to touch base."

An important component of personal well-being is autonomy—that feeling of being in control. Whenever you can exercise control over your schedule, choose to pace yourself.

If you start off your day early, choose to sack in early the night before. If you eat a heavy lunch, go easy at dinner. If you have a drink before dinner, choose to have only one. If you don't get a chance to exercise one day, hold at your level for an extra day so you don't stress your muscles.

If your work schedule on the road is heavy, find a way to do especially nice things for yourself when you can relax. Long hot baths, a trip to the manicurist during lunch, or a shampoo during your free time can do wonders to renew your spirits and refresh your body.

Finally, here's a little exercise that will help you relax when you don't have much time. Try to incorporate this into a stress management program.

"Close your eyes and imagine a favorite street, restaurant, movie theater, or shopping mall. Think about what you would do in each place. Plan how to get there and what you would wear, and imagine the sounds you would hear in each place."

Daydreaming like this involves total concentration and is a way to step away from your work day worries and cares.

Exercise Tips

Yoga stretches are excellent for starting the day with feelings of suppleness, calmness, and agility. The sunrise stretches found on page 84 accomplish this in a relaxing and controlled manner.

If you start off your day with bouncing aerobics and loud music, the day is more likely to be frenetic than when you start off with a relaxed and composed routine.

If you are in the habit of doing aerobic exercises, and if you need to keep up with them while you're on the road, it's a good idea to bring a tape and ask your instructor back home to choreograph it for you. Be careful that you have sufficient space in your hotel room to do the more active aerobics.

Skin, Hair, and Other Body Parts

One of the most taxing conditions encountered in travel is perpetual dryness. You'll want to pack a good moisturizing cream for your face and another for your body, arms, and legs.

Doing a regular cleansing routine before bedtime and remoisturizing then will go a long way toward protecting you from the dry conditions in your hotel room.

Using extra moisturizer when you fly and having a small jar in your purse or briefcase to use around your nose and a lip balm whenever you feel the dryness can help.

Your hair is also likely to take a beating when you travel. In some cities, there are no non-smoking areas in the airports. Likewise in some places there are no non-smoking areas in restaurants.

If you are exposed to cigarette or cigar smoke, and you don't smoke, you'll notice that the odors from these kinds of smoke cling to your clothing and they coat your hair.

Actions that imply ability and competence:

1. ***Rapid speech rate***
2. ***Eye contact***
3. ***Verbal fluency***
4. ***Choosing the head of the table***
5. ***Fluid gestures***
6. ***Well-moderated voice tone***

—Psychology Today

The National Women's Health Network provides information on a broad range of issues and offers referrals to women's health centers across the country. Call 202-347-1140 between 9 and 5 (eastern time).

When you're on the road, it's almost essential to wash your hair daily to keep the airborne pollutants of urban environments and other people's smoke out of your hair.

Use a gentle shampoo, and a mild conditioner if you need it, for daily hair care. Baby shampoos are often just right for handling the variety of water conditions that you encounter.

For those times when you just don't have time for a shampoo, use a little baby powder or talc on your brush and brush it thoroughly through your hair. This will serve to absorb some of the oils and can leave your hair looking clean. Don't use this method more than once before you reshampoo, however, since the powder itself can leave a residue.

Manicures and pedicures can be wonderful relaxants when you are away from home. If your schedule permits, make arrangements to have these done sometime during the middle of your stay. They can really refresh you and help maintain your self esteem. Everyone tends to feel better when they know they are taking good care of themselves.

If you should happen to lose your luggage, or forget to pack toiletries, the hotel will usually provide a temporary kit to tide you over until you can purchase some supplies. Call the front desk or the concierge and tell them what you need. They can have it delivered to your room.

Other Tips for Self-Maintenance on the Road:

1. Use a facial exfoliate as a scrub when you shower. Use it on your elbows and hands to stimulate your skin and leave it feeling clean.

2. Always moisturize your face before you put on makeup, and always clean your face before you moisturize. Use a gentle but effective cleanser at least twice a day, especially during travel since you are exposed to much more airborne pollution than at home.

3. Never expose yourself to the sun without using at least a 15 SPF sunscreen. These can be used beneath your makeup and can sometimes substitute for a moisturizer if you get one that is creamy enough. Better yet, get a moisturizer with a sunscreen already in it, especially if you will be outside where there's a lot of reflective glass or pavement.

4. Shower or bathe every day, and even twice a day, when you travel to urban areas. Cities like New York or Los Angeles are filled with noxious toxins that can reside on your skin. Even though you use moisturizer and sunscreen for protection, bathing is the only real way to get rid of the dirt.

5. Use baby shampoo as a gentle detergent for washing out lingerie that you need to wear a second time. Washing or rinsing exercise clothes and socks is a good idea before you put them on for another workout. Be sure to rinse all the shampoo out thoroughly before you hang them over the shower-curtain rod to dry.

6. A word about shoes: If you must stand on concrete floors for many hours in the day, do your legs and knees a favor and don't wear high-heeled shoes. There are many brands of shoes available today that offer both fashion and arch support. You should choose these for business travel.

PMS and Other Problems

The cycles of a woman's body can throw some women out of balance at certain times over other times. Being aware of your personal cycles of ovarian activity will help you to manage your health better during times when you are most vulnerable.

If you find your premenstrual bouts more challenging than you can handle, it's a good idea to discuss this with your gynecologist.

"The newest 'innovation' in the hotel industry is 'fragrancing.' This is the release of specific odors via the central air conditioning system."

—Sales & Marketing Management

Ask-A-Nurse is a 24-hour service that puts you in touch with a nurse in certain states. Call 1-800-535-1111 to see if it operates in the area where you're traveling.

There are some prescription products that can help. Also, there are over-the-counter preparations that are effective for some women. If you are currently doing nothing to handle your cyclic ups and downs, you may want to try them. Ask your pharmacist for recommendations.

Travel and Pregnancy

If you are a healthy woman, a normal pregnancy should not curtail reasonable travel. According to the American College of Obstetricians and Gynecologists, the best time for travel is during the second trimester when your body has adjusted to the pregnancy, but you're not so bulky that moving about is a problem.

When you travel by car, always wear a seat belt. Studies have shown that in nearly 100 percent of car crashes, the fetus recovers quickly from any pressure the seat belt exerts with no lasting injury. Seat belts with both shoulder and lap restraints are better than lap restraints only. The lap belt should be worn low on your hips, under the bulge of your abdomen.

To determine the advisability and safety of your trip, sit down with your doctor and evaluate:

1. Your obstetric history—Any complicated pregnancies or difficult deliveries?

2. Your present pregnancy—Are there any problems?

3. Personal comfort—Can you manage it and will it be acceptable?

4. Duration of your trip—More than a few days?

5. Your destination—More than 100 miles from home?

6. The quality and availability of medical and obstetrical care in your destination.

There are some absolute reasons to avoid overseas travel and many reasons to exercise caution. Your obstetrical history is important. The following conditions place women at higher risk for complications:

- Miscarriage
- Ectopic or tubal pregnancy
- Toxemia
- Premature labor
- Incompetent cervix
- Prolonged labor
- Caesarean section
- Premature ruptured membranes
- Uterine or placental abnormalities
- Hypertension
- Pelvic inflammatory disease (PID)

Here's a quick rule of thumb: If you will be far away from quick, expert medical care, and your exposure to other diseases is increased by your travel, then travel should be discouraged.

Most obstetricians advise women not to travel beyond a 100-mile radius after the 28th week. Problems after this time can include premature labor, preterm rupture of membranes, development of hypertension, phlebitis, and increased risk of uterine and placental injury from auto accidents.

Before you leave on any trip, consider an ultrasound examination to check for any problems. Have your doctor clear you medically for travel and ask for prescriptions for any medications that you may need.

Plan ahead. What will you do if an emergency arises? (See Chapter 7 for information on how and where to get emergency help.)

If you are pregnant and are planning to travel to an exotic overseas destination, the current *International Travel Health Guide,* may be helpful. It is available from Travel Medicine, Inc. at (800) 872-8633. The guide contains

The "worst" U.S. cities—according to the Environmental Protection Agency:

Ozone Level
Los Angeles
Bakersfield, CA
Fresno, CA
Houston

Carbon Monoxide
New York City
Spokane
Los Angeles
Steubenville, OH-Weirton, WV

—Traveling Healthy

New York's Lenox Hill Hospital offers Tel-Med, a collection of prerecorded health information tapes on 31 topics, ranging from stress to nutrition. Call (212) 434-3200.

complete information on immunizations and the current dangers as they relate to pregnancy.

If birth control is an issue for you, you'll want to bring protection with you. If you are on the pill and will be traveling to a high-altitude destination (15,000 feet or more), Dr. Isadore Rosenfeld says you may want to stop taking the pill. Some people may develop clots in the veins of the legs (thrombophlebitis) and the pill makes you more susceptible.

It's a good idea to be informed about sexually transmitted diseases if you plan to participate in sexual activity. Rule number one: Always, always, always insist on condom use, and also use a diaphragm and spermicidal jelly to protect yourself from venereal disease, hepatitis, and pregnancy. A good case can be made for avoiding sexual contact with casual acquaintances, but this is your personal decision.

While abstinence is your safest course of action, having good information can also help protect you. A 1989 Gallup poll revealed that 20 percent of young, single women have had three or more sex partners during the last five years without using condoms. This places them at "high risk" for AIDS. Do not be deceived, you are not at less risk than men because you are heterosexual and female. This poll concluded that "smart, rich women are fooling themselves into believing that AIDS is not an issue for them." The most rapidly growing population of HIV-positive victims is heterosexual females.

More information on AIDS and other infectious diseases is found on page 132.

6

OF INTEREST TO MEN

Protecting Yourself

Most of the dangers you confront on the road can be avoided. You don't have to drink and drive. You don't need to walk down 42nd Street in New York after 2 a.m. And you don't really need to jog in Central Park before the sun comes up. There are some dangers, however, that are more uncontrollable. You may want to know:

- What are your risks of being kidnapped, hijacked, or taken hostage when you travel abroad?
- What's the best way to reduce these risks?
- How should you react in a terrorist incident?
- When traveling to a hostile or unstable country, what rules should you follow to maintain a low profile?

Multinational corporations and their employees have increasingly become the targets of dissident groups who use them to make a political statement or to extort money.

If you must go into a situation where terrorism is a likely threat, you'll want to read *The Safe Travel Book—A Guide for the International Travelers* by Peter Savage. Another called *Managing Terrorism Risks* is available from The Ackerman Group in Miami Beach, Florida at (305) 865-0072.

To minimize your risk of kidnapping, here's a list of tips:

- Don't dress like a high-profile businessperson.
- Don't carry expensive luggage.
- Don't display tickets from U.S. airlines.

How quickly did an unattended briefcase disappear from a city park?

Dallas	*45 min.*
Denver	*30 min.*
Detroit	*50 min.*
Moscow	*7 min.*

—Condé Nast Traveler

The average manufacturing job generates four to five secondary jobs; the average retail job generates three additional jobs.

- Don't wear shirts or hats with logos of U.S. corporations on them.
- Don't carry English-language publications.
- Do take nonstop flights.
- Do send sensitive documents separately.
- Do leave a detailed travel itinerary at your office.
- Do carry medical evacuation insurance. (See Chapter 7 for details.)
- Always check U.S. State Department advisories by calling (202) 647-5225.

All of this adds up to the following: Don't call attention to yourself if you are traveling in hostile foreign countries. Do your best to blend into the surroundings. Don't play the "Ugly American" and make even the flight attendants want to knock you off. Use tact, discretion, and common sense in assessing your situation and its danger.

If you think you need more information, the U.S. State Department has teamed up with the private sector to create the Overseas Security Advisory Council (OSAC). This provides corporations doing business overseas with access to an electronic bulletin board that gives up-to-the-minute information on overseas security conditions.

You can get further security data by speaking with an OSAC analyst who can address your specific concerns. Contact OSAC by calling (202) 663-0002. Or write to them at: OSAC, DS/DSS/OSAC, P.O. Box 3590, Washington, D.C. 20007-0090.

Beyond terrorist acts, there is the danger of personal attack from today's commonplace criminals or muggers. In the event that you'll be at risk from an attack of this nature, you'll want to learn some self-defense techniques.

Today, some companies recommend that their executives play an essentially passive role if they are being mugged. Insisting that their employees carry at least $250 in cash at all times, these companies teach their people to turn over the money and to not resist and provoke a personal attack.

Use a great deal of common sense when you are in danger. Know your strengths and your weaknesses.

Of course, being physically fit is perhaps your best defense against attack. Someone whose muscle tone is excellent and whose biceps glisten is probably not going to be messed with.

If you are in less than top physical condition, you might want to learn some martial arts. Karate is one popular form of the martial arts that can be helpful. Training in karate is available at studios across the U.S. Check the Yellow Pages and look for one that is accredited.

To minimize risk, here's a list of travel tips that apply to a broader category of personal safety concerns:

1. Carefully select your areas for recreation. Ask the hotel management for information about where it is safe to walk or jog, or even swim. Never go to a beach alone.

2. Avoid small, nonscheduled airlines in lesser-developed countries.

3. Don't travel at night outside urban areas and exercise caution in certain neighborhoods of urban areas.

4. If you are out at night, stay in a group.

5. Don't hitchhike or pick up hitchhikers.

6. Don't sleep in your vehicle by the road at night.

7. Sleep only in designated camping or roadside protected areas.

8. Don't drink and drive.

9. Exercise extreme caution if you decide to drink alcohol. Don't relax by sitting on your hotel balcony with a drink.

"The worst kind of auto theft is a new phenomenon referred to as 'carjacking.' 'Bump and Run' is a variation of carjacking where thieves stage a minor rear-end accident. When the unsuspecting driver gets out to inspect the damage, one thief stages the holdup, the other takes off with the car."

—Sales & Marketing Management

"The safest car to rent is the one identical to the one you own. Differences in brands of cars can be hazardous. For example, if you rent a Bonneville but own a Honda, in a sudden rainstorm you'll find your hand on the cigarette lighter instead of the windshield wiper."

—Traveling Healthy

10. Know hotel fire safety rules and where the exits are.

11. Always lock your hotel room.

12. Keep valuables and travel documents in your room or hotel safe.

13. Avoid politically unstable regions where there is civil violence.

14. Avoid countries or regions where there is drug-related violence and drug trafficking.

15. Never purchase or use illegal drugs.

From: Rose, Dr. Stuart; 1991 International Travel Health Guide; Travel Medicine Inc. Northampton, MA.

Assertiveness Skills

If you are a typical male, you don't need any education in aggressive behavior. Your testosterone takes care of your fight-or-flight behaviors naturally.

Toning down your testosterone response might take a little training, however. The difference between aggressive behavior, which sometimes pegs you as a bully, and assertive behavior is one of tone.

The aggressive approach to getting what you want usually starts with the word "Gimme." The assertive approach sounds more like: "I'd appreciate it if you would..." or "You'd be helping me out if you...."

Depending upon your travel situation, assertive behavior will be likely to produce a more cooperative response from those whose help you need. In a restaurant, couching your special requests in polite terms and stating them very clearly can usually get you what you want without hassle. Demanding to see the manager because your steak is a little overdone usually only gets you stressed out and gives everyone with you indigestion.

Classes in assertiveness training are being given all over the country today. Their aim is not, as is often supposed, to make people more aggressive but to defuse anger before it builds up and to enhance communication between people who live and work together. Here are some of the basic assertiveness strategies:

- Experiment with simple assertions first. Choose a waiter who's just served you a cold bowl of soup before confronting your boss.

- Focus on nonverbal cues. Make eye contact. Stand straight and tall, with your head high. Don't smile nervously or giggle when you're telling someone you are angry. Don't whisper or scream; speak in a well modulated voice.

- Make sure that your timing is opportune, and choose a quiet, private place to talk.

- Don't spend so much time fretting over your words that you delay speaking up. Expressing your needs, even if imperfectly, is better than saying nothing at all.

- Remember to listen to what the other person is saying. Don't focus so much on what you're getting off your chest that you miss the apology you want.

From: The Good Health Fact Book; Readers Digest; New York: 1992.

Next time you feel like yelling at someone or calling them names, try saying, "I know you must be having a difficult time, because you didn't seem to understand my request." You might be surprised at the effect it has.

You don't have to go through a major personality change to become more assertive. Changing your daily behavior will eventually strengthen your attitudes. Being assertive gets easier each time you try. Remember, there's a fine line between aggressive behavior and self-assertion.

"It now takes an average of 4.2 calls to close a sale, compared with 5 in the early 1980s. Cellular phones, fax machines, and other technology have improved sales efficiency and productivity."

—American Demographics

The American Lung Association offers this advice for smokers on non-smoking flights:

1. When you get the urge to smoke, relax your shoulders, inhale slowly and deeply, hold your breath to the count of four, then exhale slowly. Repeat at least five times.

2. Keep your hands busy with doodling, crossword puzzles or work.

3. Leave your seat and stretch if you feel fidgety.

Asserting yourself means taking responsibility for your own feelings. Your comments should center on how you feel, "I'm angry that..." or "It really upset me that you..." or "You always take advantage of...." Once you've stated your feelings, offer constructive suggestions for how you'd like to see the situation improved.

Recognize Your Limits

Everyone has limits. Knowing how to pace yourself is particularly important when you travel. Not taking care of yourself and not getting the proper rest will take its toll.

And take this tip from *The One Minute Manager:* When you train, don't strain. Don't overdo your exercise when you're traveling, either. Even if you are staying at a hotel with a fancy fitness center, take it easy. (From: Blanchard, et al. *The One Minute Manager Gets Fit;* Blanchard Management Corp. New York: 1986.)

If you can control your schedule, try to limit your time away from home. It is better for your health. Here are some guidelines to help you feel good about yourself:

1. Choose to make a plan to achieve every day—a written list of daily goals that are realistic.

2. Approach others first—be positive.

3. Choose to have fun each day.

4. Choose to see the positive in all things.

5. Choose to be responsible for yourself.

6. Choose to be in the present. Don't dwell on the past.

7. Choose to be curious and spontaneous.

From Positive Addiction by William Glasser, M.D.; HarperCollins; New York: 1988.

Take Time for You

Find time for yourself, even if your business trip seems to you to be "critically important." Remember, many business persons give up their health to gain some wealth, only to retire early and give up their wealth to regain their health.

Taking time out for relaxation might include spending time on the golf course or playing a couple sets of tennis with a friend or colleague. Enjoying a good workout at the fitness center, having a jacuzzi bath or sauna, and relaxing in the swimming pool can refresh you.

Take advantage of the hotel's facilities as part of your management effort to take good care of yourself. But don't overdo!

You may want to be pampered in other ways. Perhaps there is a barbershop in your hotel where you can get a professional shave. Maybe you need to stop and sit down while you have your shoes shined. Read a good book or watch movies on TV back at the hotel to wind down from the day's activities.

Some things that aren't recommended include using alcohol as part of your relaxation package, using recreational drugs, or abusing your body through overexertion at your favorite sport.

When you travel you are likely to experience more than just jet lag. Frequent departures on short notice, high-pressure work schedules, job performance anxiety, traveling alone, and eating calorie-dense restaurant and airline food all work against you. You may be tempted in these circumstances to smoke, drink, and eat too much while you feel sorry for yourself. Here's our advice: don't.

Take along playing cards, crossword puzzle books, and a Walkman with your favorite tapes. Keep in close touch with the folks back home. Carry some photos of your spouse and children or close friends. Send postcards and letters. Keep a diary. Take pictures. Buy gifts and souvenirs to take home with you.

Research your destination before you go, if you have

"Only 1 in every 4,000 passengers gets bumped due to overbooking, which translates into a paltry 125,000 per year. 99.55% get their luggage at the baggage claim, the other fraction of a percentage point (2.8 million passengers) is out of luck."

—America By The Numbers

The National Exercise for Life Institute offers recorded messages on strength training, aerobic exercise, weight loss, etc. Call (800) 358-3636.

time. Do everything you can to turn the trip into an adventure. Look at it as a chance to learn and grow.

Exercise Tips

A regular exercise program promotes physical and mental health. Exercising also helps control your weight and combats insomnia. Not being fit can lower your self esteem. You can usually walk or jog anywhere and it requires no special equipment. If walking or jogging is part of your regular exercise program, you can probably enjoy it while you're away from home.

The only caution here is to check with the hotel front desk about the safety of the area where you want to walk. Ask about times you want to go and if there are any problems you need to know about. If the hotel neighborhood is not safe, find out where you can exercise in relative safety.

You may want to use a guidebook to plan walking tours of local attractions like museums or historic sites as part of your exercise program. Wear good walking shoes made by companies like Rockport that are attractive enough to go from recreational activity to business dress.

Plan ahead for any other exercise activities you want to pursue during your trip and pack the necessary equipment: bathing suit, tennis racquet, etc.

Staying in hotels that cater to travelers interested in fitness can provide you with complete workout facilities. Most major chains have fitness rooms or health clubs. See Chapter 2 for more information on exercising and the back of this book for a guide to hotel fitness facilities.

Hair, Skin, and Other Body Parts

Airplanes and overheated hotel rooms have a dehydrating effect on your skin. Bring along a heavy-duty moisturizing cream, like Vaseline Intensive Care. If you are going to be outside in the bright sun for any length of time, you'll want to protect yourself by using a sunscreen with at least an SPF (sun protection factor) of 15.

Because of the airborne pollutants found in many major cities, and because there are some people out there who still smoke, you'll probably want to shower or bathe once or twice a day while you're on the road.

You will want to wash the travel grime out of your hair at least daily. Because of the vagaries of local water supplies around the world, use a mild shampoo and possibly a mild hair conditioner if your scalp or hair tends to be dry.

Using baby shampoo for an everyday shampoo is a safe bet. Using something harsher can further damage hair already under attack by dry conditions and strange water.

Part of the standard travel kit for men should include an antifungal foot spray. If you plan on participating in activities at the hotel fitness club and you'll be showering there, your chances of getting "athlete's foot" are increased over showering at home.

If you are going to be exercising and perspiring profusely, you'll want to take along some Cruex to take care of jock itch.

While jock straps are a thing of the past for most men, if you use one, you'll want to try to wash it out after a heavy workout. Use baby shampoo as a detergent and rinse the jock strap thoroughly to be sure all the soap is out of it before you hang it to dry. This can keep it clean without doing much damage to the fabric.

Sexual Protection

Sexually transmitted diseases are a real danger if you plan to participate in sexual activity.

The number one rule: Always, always, always use a condom. A good case can be made for avoiding sexual contact with casual acquaintances, but this is your personal decision. Chapter 4 presents more information on sexually transmitted diseases and other infectious diseases.

The all-time most-requested in-room movies, according to the American Motel & Hotel Association:

1. *Pretty Woman*
2. *Home Alone*
3. *Crocodile Dundee*
4. *Sleeping With the Enemy*
5. *Rain Man*

8

WHEN YOU NEED HELP

Language

There are a number of ways to master the language of the foreign country you are visiting. Berlitz offers perhaps the most famous and most intensive program, which is available both in classrooms and on cassette tapes. You can use a Walkman to learn Spanish, French, Japanese, or almost any language spoken in the world today.

If your business requires you to be fluent in a language other than your own, however, you may want to hire a local translator. Check the telephone directory of your destination and locate the temporary help agencies. Someone at your hotel can usually help you, too. As a matter of fact, many luxury hotels have this service available through their own secretarial or services pool.

There are many publications and multi-language dictionaries on the market. Spanish-English, French-English, Chinese-English, etc., dictionaries even provide you with pronunciation aids so your rendition of the foreign language can come reasonably close.

What these books cannot do, however, is teach you how to form complete sentences. For that we recommend that you take a class at a local Berlitz center or the adult education program in your community before you go.

For those with no time for any of the above, there are electronic language translators available today. These can handle up to five different languages and can be obtained by contacting Magellan's International Travel Corporation at (800) 962-4943 in Santa Barbara, California.

The AT&T Language Line (800)628-8486 provides interpreters for 140 languages. Call the service, give them your credit-card number, the language to be translated, and the international number to be dialed. They'll place the call and help bridge the language gap. Service available 24 hours a day. Cost is $3.50 per minute plus long-distance charges.

Free information on thousands of hotels is available by fax. The TravelFax service provides up-to-date information on the amenities of participating hotels worldwide including location maps, special guest services, meeting facilities, and nearby attractions. Call (800) 891-8747.

They have a full catalog of all kinds of useful travel paraphernalia.

Probably the best and the most handy aid to handling communications in foreign languages is a phrase book. These are available at most bookstores and contain lists, usually organized by topics, of handy phrases you will undoubtedly need to know. Among these are:

- "Where is the bathroom?"
- "How much does that cost?"
- "I need a doctor."
- "Can you help me?"
- "Where is the nearest hospital?"
- "How much do I owe you?"
- "Can you get me a taxi?"

Illness and Accidents

In many parts of the world it's not easy to find good medical care. If you get sick overseas, call your regular doctor at home. If you need treatment, you can contact the nearest U.S. embassy for the names of recommended physicians. Management at some luxury hotels can also direct you to qualified doctors, even if you are not a guest. In an emergency, go to the largest hospital in the area.

As with all other travel contingencies, it's best to be prepared and "know before you go." Did you know that in China, the larger vehicle always has the right of way? If you are hit by a car there, you are considered at fault. Sounds bizarre, but there are varying customs all over the world, and if you're off to some distant city, get information before you leave. There's a list of sources at the end of this chapter to help you.

Immunizations

Immunizations may be required for travel if your destination is abroad and exotic. Usually you only need yellow fever shots, but be sure to check before you go. *The International Travel Health Guide,* published by Travel Medicine, is a good source for this kind of information.

Some immunizations come in series and hepatitis B, for example, requires 6 months. Others require that you be inoculated 4 to 6 weeks before you go.

Disease Information Hotlines

The U.S. Public Health Service Centers for Disease Control (CDC) has a 24-hour traveler's hotline at (404) 332-4559 that gives you the latest malaria advisories and vaccination requirements. You can, using a touch-tone phone, select capsule summaries of important travel-related disease information. Available options include:

- Information for physicians.
- Information on vaccination requirements and recommendations, advice on safe food and water, travelers' diarrhea, and information about various diseases and their prevention in specific areas.
- Disease outbreak bulletins.
- Publications available.
- Information on AIDS testing and foreign travel.

The Public Health Service, unlike the CDC hotline, offers telephone consultation with a travel advisor. To talk with someone directly, here are the numbers to call and the hours of operation in local time for some major U.S. cities:

Chicago: (312) 894-2960 (noon to 8 p.m.)

Honolulu: (808) 541-2552 (6 a.m. to 3 p.m.)

Los Angeles: (310) 215-2365 (6:30 a.m. to 5 p.m.)

Miami: (305) 526-2910 (4:30 a.m. to 5 p.m.)

New York: (718) 553-1685 (8 a.m. to 10 p.m.)

San Francisco: (415) 876-2872 (8 a.m. to 4 p.m.)

Seattle: (206) 553-4519 (7:30 a.m. to 5 p.m.)

"An ideal way to overcome fatigue and aches and pains and bring on relaxing sleep after long flights is a refreshing massage, say legions of travelers. Massages are especially popular and an accepted part of travel in the Far East and in some European countries."

—Traveling Healthy

The U.S. State Department, in addition to publishing world travel advisories, has a Citizens Emergency Center (CEC) in Washington at (202) 647-5225. The CEC provides assistance to American citizens in the event of illness or death while traveling outside the U.S.

Foreign Travel Publications

The Bureau of Consular Affairs, Public Affairs Staff, Room 5807, Department of State, Washington, D.C. 20520, publishes a series on travel tips for countries from the Caribbean to South Asia, the People's Republic of China, and all points in between. Do your homework and read about a destination before you go.

Coping with an illness or injury when you are away from home is often more stressful because your support structure is elsewhere. If you can stay calm, you may be able to solve the problems yourself. Check your medical travel kit first and find the supplies you packed to treat a minor infection, rash, cut, or simple sprain.

Finding a Hospital

If you have bleeding, chest or abdominal pains, or trouble breathing, find the nearest hospital. In large cities, there are often hospitals associated with medical schools where there are likely to be English-speaking doctors, as well as qualified specialists.

Ask for assistance from the hotel staff where you are staying and, if you suspect you are having a heart attack, call an ambulance. Remember, with a heart attack, early diagnosis and treatment are vital.

Always Carry Identification

The possibility of a heart attack or other emergency is a good reason to always carry identification with you, even while exercising. There are many instances where authorities have not been able to immediately notify family members when a traveler without identification has been hurt or worse.

If you are involved in an automobile or sports accident and have deep lacerations or a fracture, go immediately to a hospital. Bruises, minor scratches, and small cuts probably won't require medical attention.

If you are hospitalized, try to find out if your doctor is board-certified (or the equivalent) or has received advanced training in the United States, Canada, or Europe. Always carry a phrase book that provides medical words to help you describe your symptoms in case an English-speaking physician is not immediately available.

Call Your Home Doctor

If you are hospitalized abroad, it's a good idea to call your doctor back home for a consultation. Describe your symptoms, the history of your illness, what the diagnosis is, and the treatment. Let your doctor know if you are exposed to tropical diseases. If possible, ask your doctor to discuss your situation with the doctor treating you.

Finding a Doctor Abroad

Many hotels have doctors on call, so finding one can be as simple as calling the front desk. The U.S. embassies and consulates abroad maintain referral lists from which you can choose.

English-Speaking Doctors

Also, there is the International Association for Assistance to Travelers (IAMAT), a Canadian foundation that publishes a booklet with an extensive listing of English-speaking overseas physicians. Call IAMAT at (716) 754-4883 (their number in Lewiston, NY) or (519) 836-0102 (their headquarters in Guelph, Ontario).

Generally, sore throats, earaches, colds, diarrhea, and the flu do not need medical attention. You should have packed some remedies for these in your travel kit. See Chapter 4 for guidelines on how to deal with minor inconveniences.

Travel Clinics

Visit a travel clinic if you return home with a mysterious illness. Specialists there will be familiar with diseases rarely seen in the United States. For a directory of clinics, send a self-addressed stamped (98 cents postage) 9- by 11-inch envelope to Dr. Leonard Marcus, Traveler's Health and Immunization Services, 148 Highland Ave., Newton, MA 02165.

Travel Insurance

Several companies offer short-term health insurance for travelers. We list several companies later in this section and suggest you contact them more information. The policies provide cash in an emergency since many foreign doctors require up-front payments. Because Medicare won't pay for treatments outside the country, supplemental coverage is essential for senior travelers.

Emergency Medical Evacuation

A policy that covers emergency medical evacuation is worth considering. If appropriate care isn't available, an air ambulance will whisk you to a modern hospital. Without insurance, this service will cost you between $10,000 and $20,000. Although the likelihood that you'll need evacuation is slim, this coverage is recommended for even healthy travelers. When you must deal with a health-related emergency, "better safe than sorry."

Your credit card company may offer traveler's medical assistance as a cardholder benefit (this is other than an insurance benefit).

If you are an American Express cardholder, you can obtain the names of overseas doctors by calling the American Express Global Assist hotline at (800) 554-AMEX. From overseas, call collect to (202) 554-2639. Preferred Visa and Gold MasterCard also provide this service. Citibank Visa's Citi-Assist can be reached at (800) 332-2484 or call (202) 347-0808 from overseas.

If you have purchased a travel health policy with assistance, call the 24-hour hotline number for physician referral as listed with your documents.

Types of Travel Insurance

When buying travel insurance, be sure you understand what is NOT covered in the policy. Essentially, there are two types of travel insurance available: (1) policies that make direct payment for medical care and that provide assistance; and (2) reimbursement policies that cover emergency expenses, but not before you get treatment—

you must pay these yourself and then file a claim when you get home for reimbursement.

Some policies will pay some or all of the cost to transport you to the nearest adequate medical facility for treatment. Some policies also pay for the cost to fly you home after your medical condition has stabilized. This is called a repatriation or evacuation benefit.

To determine how much medical coverage you need, you must determine whether your own medical insurance at home will pay any amount in excess of the coverage provided by the travel policy.

If you don't have a major medical policy, then buy a travel insurance policy with higher medical benefits, such as TravMed or Health Care Abroad's $100,000 coverage. If you do carry your own major medical, then $5,000 or $10,000 is reasonable coverage since it will be enough to pay your deductible.

Some policies include the travel assistance feature mentioned above. This 24-hour telephone helpline can be of real benefit if you need a doctor and just ran out of cash or traveler's checks.

Insurance Costs

Travel insurance policies can cost from $3 to $5 per day for benefits up to $100,000. Be sure you read all the fine print so you understand clearly all the exclusions and restrictions. Some policies are only good if you are outside your home country. Others cover you if you are just 100 miles from home. There may be an upper age limit, and some don't cover sports injuries.

Also excluded may be travel to certain high-risk areas, especially if the U.S. Department of State prohibits travel to that area (as it currently does in Libya, Cuba, and Lebanon).

Starting on the following page, some companies are listed that provide direct insurance payments, plus assistance:

Direct Travel Health Insurance

TravMed
Box 10623
Baltimore, MD 21285-5225
(800)872-8633

$100,000 coverage available up to age 80.

HealthCare Abroad
243 Church St. NW
Suite 100-D
Vienna, VA 22180
(800) 237-6615 or (703) 281-9500

$100,000 coverage for up to age 76. No coverage for complications of pregnancy.

Travel Assistance International
1133 15th St. NW
Washington, DC 20005
(800) 821-2828 or (202) 331-1609

$5,000 medical benefit plus unlimited expenses for medical transport. Policy covers medical complications of pregnancy through the third trimester.

Other companies include: **Access America** at (800) 284-8300, which is located in New York City; **WorldCare Travel Assistance,** Los Angeles, at (800) 253-1877, and **International SOS** in Philadelphia at (800) 523-8930. This last company provides assistance advice and payments for medical transport. It does not pay for medical treatment, however.

Reimbursement Travel Health Insurance

Reimbursement travel health insurance is available from the following list of companies. Remember that these companies pay you after you get home and file a claim:

American Express-Travel Protection Plan
1650 Los Gamos Drive
San Rafael, CA 94903
(800) 234-0375

Benefits include $1,500 for trip cancellation, up to $100,000 evacuation, up to $10,000 illness or injury, and they cover scuba diving injuries.

Travelers Insurance Co.-Travel Pak
(800) 243-3174 or (203) 277-2318 in Connecticut

Policy pays up to $25,000 for emergency medical evacuation, depending upon your trip cancellation insurance. Medical policy covers pregnancy complications.

Mutual of Omaha-Tele-Trip Policy
Box 31685,
North Farnam St.
Omaha, NE 68131
(800) 228-9792 or (402) 345-2400

Policy covers scuba diving injuries among other full coverage aspects.

Car Insurance

If you plan to drive your own car to business in Mexico or points south, check with your local insurance agent. You'll also want to check to see which countries require local automobile insurance coverage.

Talk to your travel agent or consult *The Traveler's Handbook,* edited by Melissa Shales (Globe Pequot, 1988). This contains a myriad of useful information on every aspect of travel, including weather charts, immunization schedules, driving requirements, typical business hours, and more.

A Word About Airports

Traveler's Aid Office

If you have trouble or need assistance in an airport, there is usually a Traveler's Aid office somewhere inside the main terminal. In major U.S. cities, you can ask at any airline ticket counter and they should be able to give you directions. In foreign cities, you'll probably need to do some research to locate the help you need.

How safe is the airport where you'll land? The Department of Transportation offers a recorded message of any known threats to airlines or other public transportation systems in the U.S. or abroad. The Travel Advisory number is (800) 221-0673.

Be sure to carry a language phrase book or translating device to help communicate what you are looking for.

If you find there is no Traveler's Aid office, check with the office of Airport Security. They should be able to help. The assistance center of your travel insurance carrier is also ready to lend help for a variety of other travel-related problems.

Non-medical assistance includes travel document and ticket replacement, emergency cash transfer, emergency message center, legal assistance (like lending you bail money and helping locate a lawyer), helping you replace lost prescriptions, or helping replace a lost passport or other document.

When your insurance policy advances you bail money, be aware that you'll have to reimburse the insurer after you get home.

Ships and Boats

If your travel has you spending time on a cruise ship or drifting through France on a canal boat, be aware that the Purser on the ship should usually be your first point of contact when you need help.

If you become ill, there is usually a staff doctor on board most cruise ships. If you are on a boat, hopefully you'll be close enough to shore to get the help you need. If not, call for the captain.

Telephone Calls

The communications from ship to shore today are excellent. Just as you can make phone calls from airplanes in flight or trains on the roll, you can call with excellent voice clarity from ships to most points around the world.

In many countries today it is possible to use an express call service such as AT&T's USA Direct or MCI's Call USA.

Dialing their local access number connects you to an operator in the U.S. You can charge the call to your telephone credit card or you can call collect.

If you are calling the access number from your hotel room, you will avoid the hotel surcharge on overseas calls. Information on AT&T's service can be obtained by calling (800) 874-3000, ext. 359. For MCI, call (800) 444-4444.

Checking the Weather

There are useful sources available for checking the weather and more in countries worldwide.

The World Weather Guide by E.A. Pierce and Gordon Smith (Times Books) is available at bookstores or directly from Random House, Inc. at (800) 733-3000.

You can also call one of the 900 numbers listed below to get up-to-the-minute travel advisories and weather forecasts. The call must be made from a touch-tone phone and usually costs 95 cents a minute.

USA TODAY Weather Report (900) 555-5555

- Weather information for 650 cities worldwide
- Cites foreign country entry requirements
- Reports malaria risk advisories
- Gives U.S. dollar exchange rates
- Tells voltage requirements for appliances

American Express 1-900-WEATHER (900-932-8437)

- Gives local time, current weather, and 3-day forecasts
- Lists passport and visa entry requirements
- Gives restaurant and hotel information

"A cold is both positive and negative; sometimes the Eyes have it and sometimes the Nose."
William Lyon Phelps

"We have a choice every day regarding the attitude we will embrace for that day. I am convinced that life is 10 percent what happens to me and 90 percent how I react to it. And so it is with you... we are in charge of our attitudes."
Charles Swindoll

The Last Word

Although you can't escape the remote possibility that some unlucky incident might happen to you when you travel, you can take the steps outlined in this book to lessen that possibility.

Remember to plan your trip carefully, be reasonably cautious when you're on the road, obey common sense rules of behavior, and don't panic! Also, bear in mind that most of the world's travelers return home unharmed, so try to have the best time you can.

For more information on health and travel, try the 8-page *Traveling Healthy* newsletter; published 6 times a year. A subscription is $24 a year. *Traveling Healthy,* 108-48 70th Road, Forest Hills, NY 11375.

If you're traveling abroad, you'll want the current edition of *The International Travel Health Guide,* by Stuart Rose, M.D., available from Travel Medicine, Inc., 351 Pleasant St., Suite 312, Northampton, MA 01060.

Other good sources of information to help you prepare for travel include:

- *The Diabetic Traveler Newsletter,* Box 8223 RW, Stamford, CT 06905. A 6-page quarterly for an annual subscription of $18.95. A sample issue, plus business card-sized insulin adjustment guide for air travel through multiple time zones, is available for $3.
- *Consumer Reports Travel Letter;* call (800) 525-0643 for subscription information.
- *World Business Travel Guide* (Summerhill Press, Ltd. Toronto, 1987). This contains useful statistics on demographics, weather, hotels, airlines, and medical facilities in over 200 countries.

APPENDIX: HOTELS WITH EXERCISE FACILITIES

The following list of hotels includes only those hotels that met a minimum criterion of at least three of the following amenities: pool, whirlpool or hot tub, sauna, steam room, exercise equipment, exercise room with instructor, weights, weight machines, stair machine, stationary bicycles, treadmills, rowers or rowing machines, tennis, jogging trail, or golf.

When making reservations, be sure to check that these facilities are still available and learn if additional exercise outlets may be available nearby if not on hotel premises. All information based upon best available sources.

✗–available at a nearby location.
✱–local health club privileges.

	Pool	Whirlpool	Hot tub	Sauna	Steam room	Exercise equipment	Exercise room	Instructor	Weights	Weight machine	Stair machine	Stationary bicycle	Treadmill	Rowing machine	Jogging trail	Tennis	Lighted tennis courts	Golf	Putting green	Driving range
ALBANY																				
The Desmond	✓(2)	✓		✓		✓						✓		✓						
Hilton		✓				✓			✓		✓									
Holiday Inn, Turf	✓(2)	✓		✓													✓			
Marriott		✓		✓		✓			✓			✓								
ALBUQUERQUE																				
Barcelona Court	✓(2)	✓		✓																
Courtyard	✓	✓				✓			✓			✓								
Doubletree	✓					✓			✓			✓								
Hilton Inn	✓(2)	✓		✓												✓				
Holiday Inn (pyramid)	✓	✓		✓		✓			✓			✓								
Holiday Inn (midtown)	✓	✓		✓		✓			✓			✓								
Hyatt Regency	✓			✓		✓			✓			✓								
Marriott	✓	✓		✓		✓			✓			✓								
Ramada Classic	✓	✓		✓		✓				✓		✓				✗		✗		
ATLANTA																				
Atlanta Penta	✓					✓			✓			✓								
Courtyard	✓	✓				✓			✓			✓								
Courtyard (north)	✓	✓				✓			✓			✓								
Doubletree	✓	✓		✓												✓		✓		
Embassy Suites	✓(2)	✓		✓		✓			✓			✓								
Hilton	✓(2)	✓		✓			✓	✓		✓		✓					✓			
Hilton & Towers	✓	✓		✓			✓	✓		✓		✓				✓				
Holiday Inn		✓		✓		✓				✓		✓								
Hotel Nikko				✓		✓						✓	✓			✓		✓		
Hyatt Regency	✓	✓		✓	✓	✓			✓			✓								
J.W. Marriott	✓	✓		✓			✓	✓	✓			✓								
Marriott Marquis	✓	✓		✓			✓	✓		✓		✓								
Ramada (renaissance)	✓	✓		✓		✓	✓	✓				✓								
Ritz-Carlton		✓		✓		✓				✓		✓				✓		✓		
Sheraton (colony square)	✓	✓		✓	✓		✓	✓	✓			✓								
Stouffer Waverly	✓(2)	✓		✓	✓		✓	✓		✓		✓								
Wyndham (midtown)	✓	✓		✓		✓	✓	✓	✓			✓								

✗–available at a nearby location.
✱–local health club privileges.

	Pool	Whirlpool	Hot tub	Sauna	Steam room	Exercise equipment	Exercise room	Instructor	Weights	Weight machine	Stair machine	Stationary bicycle	Treadmill	Rowing machine	Jogging trail	Tennis	Lighted tennis courts	Golf	Putting green	Driving range
AUSTIN, TX																				
Doubletree	✓	✓		✓		✓			✓			✓								
Embassy Suites	✓			✓		✓			✓			✓								
Four Seasons	✓	✓		✓			✓	✓	✓			✓								
Guest Quarters	✓	✓		✓		✓				✓		✓								
Hawthorn Suites✱	✓	✓																		
Holiday Inn (townlake)	✓	✓		✓		✓					✓	✓								
Hilton (north)						✓						✓	✓							
Marriot (at the capitol)	✓	✓		✓		✓				✓		✓								
Radisson Plaza	✓	✓		✓		✓			✓			✓								
Stouffer Austin	✓(2)	✓		✓		✓			✓			✓								
BALTIMORE																				
Best Western (BWI airport)	✓	✓		✓		✓				✓		✓								
Clarion (harrison's pier 5)						✓				✓		✓								
Embassy Suites	✓	✓		✓	✓															
Guest Quarters (airport)	✓	✓		✓		✓			✓			✓								
Harbor Court	✓	✓		✓			✓	✓		✓		✓				✓				
Hilton Inn	✓	✓					✓	✓		✓		✓				✓				
Hyatt Regency	✓	✓		✓	✓		✓	✓		✓		✓				✓				
Marriot	✓	✓		✓			✓	✓	✓			✓								
Omni (inner harbor)	✓					✓			✓			✓								
Radisson (lord baltimore)		✓		✓		✓				✓		✓								
Sheraton (inner harbor)				✓		✓						✓	✓							
Stouffer (harbor place)	✓	✓				✓				✓		✓				✓				
Tremont Plaza	✓			✓		✓				✓		✓								
BILLINGS																				
Holiday Inn Plaza		✓		✓		✓						✓		✓						
Radisson Northern						✓				✓		✓								
Ramada Inn	✓	✓		✓																
Sheraton	✓	✓		✓			✓	✓			✓	✓								
BIRMINGHAM																				
Courtyard		✓				✓				✓		✓								
Crown Sterling	✓				✓	✓			✓			✓								

✗–available at a nearby location.
✱–local health club privileges.

	Pool	Whirlpool	Hot tub	Sauna	Steam room	Exercise equipment	Exercise room	Instructor	Weights	Weight machine	Stair machine	Stationary bicycle	Treadmill	Rowing machine	Jogging trail	Tennis	Lighted tennis courts	Golf	Putting green	Driving range
Holiday Inn (airport)	✓					✓			✓			✓								
Ramada Inn (airport)	✓					✓				✓		✓								
Sheraton (civic center)	✓	✓		✓		✓						✓	✓							
Wynfrey (riverchase galleria)	✓				✓	✓			✓			✓								
BISMARK																				
Radisson Inn	✓	✓		✓		✓			✓			✓								
BOISE																				
Boise Park Suite	✓	✓				✓			✓			✓								
Doubletree Club	✓					✓			✓			✓								
Holiday Inn	✓(2)					✓						✓		✓						
Red Lion Hotel (riverside)	✓	✓				✓				✓		✓								
BOSTON																				
Boston Harbor	✓	✓		✓			✓	✓		✓		✓								
Boston Park Plaza ✱	✱					✓			✓			✓								
Four Seasons	✓	✓		✓		✓			✓			✓								
Guest Quarters Suites	✓	✓		✓																
Hilton (back bay)	✓			✓		✓			✓			✓								
Holiday Inn✱ (gov. cntr.)	✓					✓			✓			✓								
Marriot (copley place)	✓	✓		✓	✓		✓	✓	✓			✓								
Marriot (long wharf)	✓	✓		✓		✓			✓			✓								
Meridien	✓						✓	✓	✓				✓							
Ramada (airport)	✓					✓				✓	✓									
Ritz-Carlton ✱				✓			✓	✓	✓			✓								
Sheraton Boston	✓	✓				✓			✓			✓								
Westin (copley place)	✓	✓		✓			✓	✓	✓			✓								
BURLINGTON																				
Howard Johnson	✓	✓		✓		✓			✓			✓								
Residence Inn	✓	✓				✓				✓		✓								
Sheraton Hotel	✓	✓					✓	✓	✓			✓				✗				
CASPER																				
Days Inn	✓	✓		✓																
Holiday Inn	✓	✓		✓		✓		✓					✓							

✗–available at a nearby location.
✱–local health club privileges.

	Pool	Whirlpool	Hot tub	Sauna	Steam room	Exercise equipment	Exercise room	Instructor	Weights	Weight machine	Stair machine	Stationary bicycle	Treadmill	Rowing machine	Jogging trail	Tennis	Lighted tennis courts	Golf	Putting green	Driving range
CHARLESTON, SC																				
Marriott	✓	✓				✓			✓			✓				✓		✱		
Omni (charleston place)	✓	✓		✓	✓		✓	✓	✓			✓				✱		✱		
Wild Dunes	✓	✓															✓	✓	✓	✓
CHARLESTON, WV																				
Holiday Inn	✓					✓			✓			✓								
Marriott (town center)	✓	✓		✓		✓			✓			✓								
CHICAGO																				
Drake Hotel ✱						✓					✓			✓		✱				
Embassy Suites	✓	✓		✓		✓			✓			✓								
Four Seasons ✱		✓					✓	✓		✓		✓								
Hilton & Towers		✓		✓			✓	✓	✓			✓								
Holiday Inn✱ (city center)	✓															✱				
Hotel Nikko Chicago				✓			✓	✓	✓			✓								
Hotel Sofitel (o'hare)	✓			✓		✓			✓			✓								
Hyatt Regency Suites	✓	✓		✓		✓				✓		✓				✱				
Hyatt Regency (o'hare)	✓			✓	✓	✓			✓			✓								
Inter-Continental	✓			✓			✓	✓		✓		✓				✱				
Marriot Suites	✓	✓		✓		✓				✓		✓								
McCormick Center	✓	✓		✓	✓		✓	✓	✓			✓				✱				
Midway Inn (airport)						✓			✓			✓								
Palmer House Hilton	✓	✓		✓	✓		✓	✓	✓			✓								
Ramada Hotel (o'hare)	✓	✓		✓		✓			✓			✓				✓		✓		
Ritz-Carlton		✓		✓	✓		✓	✓	✓			✓				✱				
Stouffer Riviere		✓		✓		✓				✓		✓				✱				
Westin (o'hare)	✓	✓		✓			✓	✓	✓			✓								
Westin (chicago)				✓	✓		✓	✓	✓			✓								
CLEVELAND																				
Clarion (east)	✓			✓		✓		✓					✓							
Embassy Suites	✓	✓		✓		✓			✓			✓								
Harley Hotel (east)	✓(2)			✓		✓			✓			✓								
Harley Hotel (south)	✓	✓			✓											✓				
Hilton (south)	✓	✓		✓		✓			✓			✓				✓				

✗–available at a nearby location.
✱–local health club privileges.

	Pool	Whirlpool	Hot tub	Sauna	Steam room	Exercise equipment	Exercise room	Instructor	Weights	Weight machine	Stair machine	Stationary bicycle	Treadmill	Rowing machine	Jogging trail	Tennis	Lighted tennis courts	Golf	Putting green	Driving range
Marriott (airport)	✓	✓		✓		✓			✓			✓								
Marriott (east)						✓				✓			✓							
Quality Hotel	✓					✓				✓		✓								
Quality Inn (east)	✓	✓		✓		✓			✓			✓								
Radisson Inn	✓	✓		✓		✓				✓		✓								
Radisson Inn (airport)	✓	✓		✓		✓				✓				✓						
Radisson Plaza	✓	✓					✓	✓	✓			✓					✓			
Ritz-Carlton	✓	✓		✓			✓	✓		✓		✓								
Sheraton (city center)						✓				✓		✓								
Stouffer Tower	✓			✓		✓			✓			✓								
CONCORD, NH																				
Comfort Inn	✓	✓		✓																
Ramada Inn	✓	✓		✓		✓						✓	✓							
DALLAS																				
The Adolphus ✱						✓				✓		✓				✱		✱		
Bristol Suites	✓	✓				✓			✓			✓								
Clarion ✱						✓					✓	✓								
Courtyard	✓	✓				✓			✓			✓								
Crescent Court		✓		✓	✓		✓	✓	✓			✓				✱		✱		
Doubletree (park west)	✓	✓		✓		✓				✓		✓								
Embassy (no. central)	✓	✓		✓	✓	✓						✓		✓						
Fairmont ✱	✓															✱		✱		
Four Seasons Resort	✓	✓		✓	✓		✓	✓		✓		✓				✓		✓		
Hilton DFW (conf. center)	✓(2)	✓			✓		✓	✓	✓			✓				✓		✱		✓
Holiday Inn (airport n.)	✓					✓				✓		✓								
Holiday Inn (crowne plaza)	✓	✓		✓		✓			✓			✓								
Holiday Inn (LBJ n.e.)				✓		✓				✓			✓							
Hyatt Regency	✓	✓		✓	✓	✓			✓			✓								
Hyatt Regency DFW	✓			✓	✓		✓	✓	✓			✓				✓		✓		✓
Loew's Anatole	✓(2)	✓		✓	✓		✓	✓	✓			✓					✓			
Marriott Quorum	✓	✓		✓		✓			✓			✓				✱		✱		
Marriott DFW	✓	✓		✓			✓	✓	✓			✓				✱		✱		
Radisson Stemmons	✓	✓				✓			✓			✓								

✗–available at a nearby location.
✱–local health club privileges.

	Pool	Whirlpool	Hot tub	Sauna	Steam room	Exercise equipment	Exercise room	Instructor	Weights	Weight machine	Stair machine	Stationary bicycle	Treadmill	Rowing machine	Jogging trail	Tennis	Lighted tennis courts	Golf	Putting green	Driving range
Radisson Central ✱	✓	✓		✓																
Ramada	✓			✓		✓			✓			✓								
Sheraton Grand DFW	✓	✓		✓		✓			✓		✓									
Stouffer Dallas	✓	✓		✓	✓	✓			✓			✓								
DENVER																				
Comfort Inn (airport)	✓					✓			✓			✓								
Courtyard	✓	✓				✓				✓		✓								
Doubletree	✓	✓				✓					✓	✓								
Embassy (suites)	✓	✓		✓		✓					✓	✓								
Embassy (tech center) ✱	✓	✓		✓		✓				✓		✓								
Hilton (denver south)	✓			✓		✓				✓		✓								
Holiday Inn (I-70E)	✓	✓		✓		✓				✓		✓								
Hyatt Regency (tech center)	✓	✓		✓		✓			✓			✓								
Marriott (city center)	✓	✓		✓			✓	✓		✓		✓								
Marriott (s.e.)	✓(2)	✓				✓					✓	✓								
Oxford				✓	✓		✓	✓		✓		✓								
Radisson	✓	✓		✓	✓	✓			✓			✓								
Radisson South ✱	✓	✓														✱				
Red Lion	✓	✓		✓		✓				✓		✓								
Residence Inn ✱ *(d. town)*	✓	✓				✓			✓			✓								
Sheraton (tech center)	✓(2)	✓		✓	✓	✓			✓			✓								
Sheraton (west)	✓	✓		✓	✓		✓	✓		✓		✓								
Stouffer Concourse	✓(2)	✓			✓		✓	✓		✓		✓								
Westin (tabor center)	✓	✓		✓		✓				✓		✓								
DES MOINES																				
Crystal Inn	✓	✓		✓		✓				✓		✓							✓	
Embassy Suites (river)	✓	✓		✓		✓				✓		✓								
Executive Inn	✓	✓		✓		✓			✓			✓								
Fort Des Moines	✓	✓		✓		✓				✓		✓								
Holiday Inn (south)	✓	✓		✓																
Holiday Inn (university)	✓	✓		✓		✓			✓			✓								
Marriott	✓	✓		✓		✓			✓			✓								
Residence Inn ✱	✓	✓				✓					✓	✓								

✗–available at a nearby location.
✱–local health club privileges.

	Pool	Whirlpool	Hot tub	Sauna	Steam room	Exercise equipment	Exercise room	Instructor	Weights	Weight machine	Stair machine	Stationary bicycle	Treadmill	Rowing machine	Jogging trail	Tennis	Lighted tennis courts	Golf	Putting green	Driving range
Sheraton Inn	✓	✓		✓																
DETROIT																				
Courtyard	✓	✓				✓			✓			✓								
Embassy Suites	✓	✓		✓		✓			✓			✓								
Georgian Inn	✓	✓										✓	✓							
Hilton Suites	✓	✓				✓				✓		✓								
Holiday Inn (fairlane)	✓(2)	✓		✓		✓					✓	✓								
Holiday Inn (livonia w.)	✓	✓		✓		✓			✓			✓							✓	
Marriott ✱	✓	✓		✓		✓			✓			✓								
Marriott (livonia) ✱	✓	✓		✓		✓			✓			✓								
Marriott (romulus)	✓	✓				✓				✓		✓								
Omni International	✓	✓		✓			✓	✓	✓			✓				✓				
Radisson	✓	✓				✓			✓			✓						✱		
Radisson (town center)	✓	✓		✓		✓			✓			✓								
River Place Inn	✓	✓		✓			✓		✓				✓			✓				
Sheraton ✱	✓	✓				✓				✓		✓				✓				
Westin (renaissance center)	✓			✓			✓	✓	✓			✓								
HARTFORD																				
The Goodwin Hotel						✓				✓		✓								
Sheraton	✓	✓		✓		✓				✓		✓								
HOUSTON																				
Allen Park Inn	✓	✓		✓		✓			✓			✓								
Doubletree ✱	✓			✓																
Four Seasons	✓	✓		✓		✓						✓		✓						
Hilton (westchase)	✓	✓		✓		✓			✓			✓								
Hilton (houston plaza)	✓	✓		✓			✓	✓	✓			✓								
Hilton (nassau bay)	✓	✓				✓			✓			✓								
Hilton (brookhollow)	✓	✓		✓		✓			✓			✓								
Holiday Inn (crowne plaza)	✓	✓	✓	✓		✓			✓			✓								
Hotel Sofitel	✓	✓		✓		✓				✓		✓								
Houstonian	✓(2)	✓		✓			✓	✓	✓			✓					✓	✱		
Hyatt Regency	✓					✓			✓			✓								
J.W. Marriot (houston)	✓	✓		✓	✓		✓	✓	✓			✓								

✗–available at a nearby location.
✱–local health club privileges.

	Pool	Whirlpool	Hot tub	Sauna	Steam room	Exercise equipment	Exercise room	Instructor	Weights	Weight machine	Stair machine	Stationary bicycle	Treadmill	Rowing machine	Jogging trail	Tennis	Lighted tennis courts	Golf	Putting green	Driving range
Marriott (airport)	✓			✓		✓					✓		✓							
Marriott (astrodome)	✓					✓				✓		✓								
Omni (houston)	✓(2)	✓		✓			✓	✓	✓			✓				✓				
Ramada ✱	✓			✓		✓			✓		✓									
Residence Inn	✓	✓				✓			✓			✓								
Ritz-Carlton (houston) ✱	✓	✓					✓		✓		✓									
Sheraton (astrodome)	✓(3)			✓		✓			✓					✓						
Stouffer Presidente	✓			✓		✓			✓			✓								
Westin Gallaria ✱	✓																✓		✓	
INDIANAPOLIS																				
Adam's Mark	✓(2)	✓		✓		✓			✓			✓								
Courtyard	✓	✓				✓				✓		✓								
Guest Quarters Suites	✓	✓				✓				✓		✓								
Holiday Inn (north)	✓	✓		✓	✓														✓	
Holiday Inn (union sta.)		✓		✓		✓						✓		✓						
Hyatt Regency	✓					✓				✓		✓								
Marriott	✓	✓				✓			✓			✓				*		*	✓	
Omni Severin	✓	✓		✓		✓				✓		✓								
Radisson Plaza/Suites ✱	✓	✓		✓																
Westin ✱	✓	✓																		
Wyndham Garden	✓	✓				✓			✓			✓								
JACKSON, MS																				
Edison Walthall	✓	✓				✓			✓			✓								
Ramada (renaissance) ✱	✓	✓														*		*		✓
KANSAS CITY																				
Adam's Mark	✓(2)	✓		✓			✓	✓	✓			✓				✓				
Allis Plaza	✓			✓			✓	✓	✓			✓				✓				
Courtyard	✓	✓				✓			✓			✓								
Doubletree	✓	✓		✓		✓				✓		✓						✓	✓	✓
Embassy Suites	✓	✓		✓																
Hilton (airport plaza)	✓(2)	✓		✓			✓	✓	✓			✓					✓			
Holiday Inn (crowne plaza)	✓	✓					✓	✓		✓		✓								
Hyatt (crowne center)	✓	✓		✓	✓		✓	✓	✓			✓					✓			

✗–available at a nearby location.
✱–local health club privileges.

	Pool	Whirlpool	Hot tub	Sauna	Steam room	Exercise equipment	Exercise room	Instructor	Weights	Weight machine	Stair machine	Stationary bicycle	Treadmill	Rowing machine	Jogging trail	Tennis	Lighted tennis courts	Golf	Putting green	Driving range
Marriott (airport)	✓	✓		✓	✓	✓			✓			✓				✱		✱		
Marriott (overland park)	✓	✓		✓		✓			✓			✓								
Marriott Suites ✱	✓	✓				✓				✓				✓						
Park Place	✓			✓		✓			✓			✓					✓			
Ritz-Carlton (kansas city)	✓			✓	✓	✓			✓			✓								
Westin (crowne center)	✓	✓		✓	✓		✓	✓	✓			✓					✓		✓	
LAS VEGAS																				
Alexis Park Resort	✓(3)	✓		✓	✓	✓			✓			✓					✓	✱		
Bally's	✓	✓		✓	✓	✓			✓			✓					✓			
Caesar's Palace	✓(2)	✓		✓	✓	✓				✓		✓				✓				
Desert Inn	✓	✓		✓	✓		✓	✓	✓			✓					✓	✓	✓	✓
Golden Nugget	✓	✓		✓	✓	✓				✓		✓								
Harrah's	✓	✓		✓		✓			✓			✓								
Hilton	✓	✓		✓		✓			✓			✓					✓	✱	✓	
Hilton (flamington)	✓(2)	✓		✓	✓		✓	✓		✓		✓				✱				
Mirage	✓(2)					✓	✓	✓				✓								
Rio Suite Hotel	✓					✓			✓			✓								
Riviera	✓	✓		✓	✓	✓			✓			✓								
LITTLE ROCK																				
Courtyard	✓	✓		✓		✓			✓			✓								
Excelsior		✓				✓			✓			✓								
Holiday Inn (west)	✓	✓		✓		✓			✓			✓								
Master's Lodge						✓			✓			✓								
LOS ANGELES																				
Beverly Plaza	✓	✓		✓		✓			✓			✓								
Biltmore	✓			✓		✓			✓			✓								
Century Plaza ✱	✓	✓														✱				
Checkers Kempinski	✓	✓		✓	✓		✓	✓		✓		✓								
Four Seasons	✓	✓					✓	✓	✓			✓				✱		✱		
Hilton & Towers	✓					✓				✓		✓								
Hilton (universal city)	✓	✓				✓			✓			✓								
Holiday Inn (crowne plaza) ✱	✓	✓		✓																
Holiday Inn (conv. center)	✓			✓		✓						✓	✓							

✗–available at a nearby location.
✱–local health club privileges.

	Pool	Whirlpool	Hot tub	Sauna	Steam room	Exercise equipment	Exercise room	Instructor	Weights	Weight machine	Stair machine	Stationary bicycle	Treadmill	Rowing machine	Jogging trail	Tennis	Lighted tennis courts	Golf	Putting green	Driving range
Hollywood Roosevelt	✓	✓				✓				✓		✓								
Hotel Nikko (beverly hills)							✓	✓		✓		✓				✱		✱		
Hotel Sofitel (ma maison)	✓					✓				✓		✓				✱				
Hyatt Regency ✱		✓				✓			✓			✓								
J.W. Marriott (cent. city)	✓(2)	✓		✓	✓		✓	✓		✓		✓				✱		✱		
Marriott (airport)	✓	✓				✓			✓			✓								
Mondrian	✓	✓		✓		✓			✓			✓								
Peninsula (beverly hills)	✓	✓		✓			✓	✓		✓			✓			✱		✱		
Regency (beverly wilshire)	✓	✓		✓	✓	✓			✓			✓						✱		
Sheraton Universal ✱						✓					✓									
Stouffer (concourse-L)	✓	✓		✓			✓	✓	✓			✓								
Sunset Marquis	✓(2)	✓		✓		✓			✓			✓								
Westwood Marquis	✓(2)			✓	✓	✓			✓			✓								
LOUISVILLE																				
Courtyard	✓	✓				✓			✓			✓								
Executive Inn	✓(2)			✓			✓	✓	✓			✓								
Holiday Inn	✓	✓		✓		✓				✓		✓								
Hyatt Regency ✱	✓	✓																		
Radisson ✱	✓	✓				✓			✓			✓								
MIAMI																				
Courtyard	✓	✓				✓				✓		✓								
Crown Sterling ✱	✓	✓																		
Don Shula's Hotel	✓(2)	✓		✓	✓		✓	✓	✓			✓				✓		✓	✓	
Doral Resort	✓	✓			✓		✓	✓	✓			✓				✓		✓		
Grand Bay	✓	✓		✓		✓			✓			✓								
Hilton & Marina	✓	✓		✓		✓			✓			✓					✓	✱		
Holiday Inn (le jeune)	✓	✓		✓		✓			✓			✓								
Marriott	✓	✓(2)				✓			✓			✓								
Marriott (biscayne bay)	✓	✓					✓	✓		✓			✓				✱			
Marriott (dadeland)	✓	✓		✓		✓			✓			✓				✱		✱		
Miami Int'l Hotel (air)	✓	✓			✓	✓			✓			✓								
Mayfair House ✱	✓		✓																	
Occidental Parc	✓					✓			✓			✓								

✗–available at a nearby location.
✱–local health club privileges.

	Pool	Whirlpool	Hot tub	Sauna	Steam room	Exercise equipment	Exercise room	Instructor	Weights	Weight machine	Stair machine	Stationary bicycle	Treadmill	Rowing machine	Jogging trail	Tennis	Lighted tennis courts	Golf	Putting green	Driving range
Omni International✱	✓															✱		✱		
Radisson (mart plaza)	✓	✓		✓	✓		✓	✓	✓			✓					✓			
Sheraton (river house)	✓	✓		✓		✓			✓			✓					✓	✱		
Sofitel	✓	✓		✓		✓			✓			✓					✓	✱		
Turnberry Isle Resort	✓(3)	✓		✓	✓		✓	✓	✓			✓				✓		✓	✓	
MEMPHIS																				
Courtyard	✓	✓				✓			✓			✓								
Days Inn	✓					✓				✓		✓								
Embassy Suites	✓	✓		✓		✓			✓			✓								
French Quarter	✓	✓				✓			✓			✓								
Holiday Inn (crowne plaza)	✓	✓		✓		✓			✓			✓								
Homewood Suites	✓	✓				✓			✓			✓								
Marriott	✓(2)	✓		✓		✓			✓			✓								
Memphis Hotel (air)	✓(2)			✓		✓			✓			✓					✱			
Peabody	✓	✓		✓	✓		✓	✓	✓			✓								
Radisson	✓	✓		✓		✓				✓		✓								
Radisson (ridgeway)	✓					✓				✓		✓								
Residence Inn	✓	✓														✓				
MINNEAPOLIS																				
Best Western (canterbury)	✓	✓		✓		✓			✓			✓								
Best Western (thunderbird)	✓(2)	✓		✓		✓			✓			✓								
Holiday Inn (airport)	✓	✓		✓		✓			✓			✓								
Holiday Inn (metrodome)	✓					✓			✓			✓								
Hyatt Regency ✱	✓																			
Luxeford		✓		✓		✓			✓			✓								
Marriott (city center)✱		✓		✓																
Marriott (southwest)	✓	✓		✓		✓				✓		✓								
Radisson (hotel - conference)	✓	✓		✓			✓	✓		✓		✓					✓			
Radisson (minnetonka)✱	✓																			
Radisson Plaza		✓		✓			✓	✓	✓			✓								
Radisson South	✓	✓		✓		✓			✓			✓								
Registry	✓	✓		✓		✓			✓		✓									
Sheraton (airport)	✓	✓				✓						✓								

✗–available at a nearby location.
✱–local health club privileges.

	Pool	Whirlpool	Hot tub	Sauna	Steam room	Exercise equipment	Exercise room	Instructor	Weights	Weight machine	Stair machine	Stationary bicycle	Treadmill	Rowing machine	Jogging trail	Tennis	Lighted tennis courts	Golf	Putting green	Driving range
Sheraton Park Place	✓	✓		✓		✓			✓			✓								
Sofitel	✓			✓		✓			✓			✓								
NEW ORLEANS																				
Clarion (new orleans)	✓	✓				✓			✓			✓								
Dauphine	✓	✓				✓			✓			✓								
Doubletree	✓					✓			✓			✓								
Fairmont ✱	✓					✓			✓				✓				✓			
Hilton Riverside ✱	✓(2)	✓		✓		✓			✓			✓				✓				
Holiday Inn (crowne plaza)	✓					✓			✓			✓								
Hyatt Regency	✓					✓			✓				✓							
Inter-Continental	✓					✓				✓		✓								
Marriott	✓			✓		✓			✓			✓								
Omni Royal	✓	✓				✓			✓			✓								
Royal Sonesta	✓					✓				✓		✓								
Sheraton	✓					✓				✓		✓								
Westin Canal Place ✱	✓															✱		✱	✓	✓
NEW YORK CITY																				
Carlyle				✓	✓		✓	✓	✓			✓								
Courtyard		✓				✓				✓		✓								
Doral Court ✱						✓			✓			✓								
Doral Inn				✓		✓				✓		✓								
Essex House (hotel nikko)				✓	✓		✓	✓		✓		✓								
Four Seasons		✓		✓			✓	✓		✓		✓								
Hilton (rockefeller center)				✓			✓	✓	✓			✓								
Holiday Inn (la guardia) ✱	✓	✓		✓			✓	✓		✓		✓								
Holiday Inn (midtown)	✓			✓	✓		✓	✓		✓		✓								
Holiday Inn (JFK)	✓	✓		✓		✓					✓	✓								
Inter-Continental				✓	✓		✓	✓		✓		✓								
Marriott (financial center)	✓			✓		✓				✓		✓								
Marriott (la guardia)		✓		✓			✓	✓		✓		✓								
Marriott Marquis		✓		✓	✓	✓			✓			✓								
Marriott (newark airport)	✓	✓		✓		✓			✓			✓								
Mayfair Baglioni						✓			✓			✓		✓						

✗–available at a nearby location.
✱–local health club privileges.

	Pool	Whirlpool	Hot tub	Sauna	Steam room	Exercise equipment	Exercise room	Instructor	Weights	Weight machine	Stair machine	Stationary bicycle	Treadmill	Rowing machine	Jogging trail	Tennis	Lighted tennis courts	Golf	Putting green	Driving range
Peninsula	✓	✓		✓	✓		✓	✓		✓		✓								
Pierre ✱	✱						✓	✓				✓	✓							
Radisson (newark airport)	✓	✓				✓			✓			✓								
Ritz-Carlton						✓						✓	✓							
Sheraton & Towers		✓					✓	✓		✓		✓								
The St. Regis Hotel				✓		✓				✓		✓								
U.N. Plaza Park (hyatt)				✓			✓	✓	✓			✓				✓				
Vista (newark airport)	✓	✓		✓		✓				✓		✓								
Waldorf Astoria					✓		✓			✓		✓								
Westbury				✓		✓						✓	✓							
NORFOLK																				
Hilton (norfollk airport)	✓	✓		✓		✓			✓			✓					✓			
Marriott Waterside	✓	✓		✓		✓				✓			✓							
Quality Inn (lake wright)	✓															✓		✓	✓	✓
Ramada Inn	✓					✓						✓		✓						
OKLAHOMA CITY																				
Best Western (saddleback)	✓	✓		✓		✓			✓			✓								
Courtyard	✓	✓		✓		✓			✓			✓								
Embassy Suites	✓	✓		✓	✓	✓			✓			✓								
Hilton (n.w.)	✓					✓			✓			✓								
Holiday Inn (airport west)	✓(2)	✓		✓		✓			✓			✓								
Holiday Inn (n. I-35)	✓	✓		✓													✓			
Marriott ✱	✓					✓			✓			✓								
Radisson	✓(4)	✓		✓		✓			✓			✓				✓			✓	
Residence Inn ✱	✓	✓														✓				
The Waterford	✓	✓		✓			✓	✓	✓			✓								
OMAHA																				
Best Western (omaha inn)	✓	✓		✓		✓			✓			✓								
Best Western Central	✓	✓		✓																
Best Western (new tower)	✓	✓		✓		✓			✓		✓									
Embassy Suites	✓	✓		✓																
Marriott	✓	✓		✓		✓			✓			✓								
Radisson		✓		✓		✓			✓			✓								

✗–available at a nearby location.
✻–local health club privileges.

	Pool	Whirlpool	Hot tub	Sauna	Steam room	Exercise equipment	Exercise room	Instructor	Weights	Weight machine	Stair machine	Stationary bicycle	Treadmill	Rowing machine	Jogging trail	Tennis	Lighted tennis courts	Golf	Putting green	Driving range
Ramada	✓	✓		✓																
Red Lion Inn	✓	✓		✓	✓	✓			✓			✓								
Residence Inn ✻	✓	✓														✓				
Sheraton Inn	✓	✓		✓																
ORLANDO																				
Buena Vista Palace	✓(3)	✓		✓		✓			✓			✓					✓	✻	✓	✓
Courtyard	✓	✓				✓			✓			✓								
Delta Resort (orlando)	✓(3)	✓		✓													✓	✻		✓
Disney Beach Club	✓(2)	✓		✓	✓		✓	✓		✓		✓					✓	✻		
Disney Contemporary	✓(2)			✓			✓	✓	✓			✓					✓	✻		
Grand Floridian	✓	✓			✓		✓	✓		✓		✓				✓		✻		
Polynesian Resort ✻	✓(2)																✓	✻		
Village Resort	✓(6)					✓		✓			✓						✓	✻	✓	✓
Disney Yacht Club	✓(4)	✓		✓	✓		✓	✓		✓		✓					✓	✻		
Dixie Landings	✓(8)	✓															✓	✻	✓	✓
Embassy Suites	✓	✓		✓	✓															
Embassy Resort	✓(2)	✓		✓		✓				✓		✓					✓	✻	✓	✓
Grosvenor Resort	✓(2)																✓´	✻	✓	✓
Guest Quarters	✓	✓				✓			✓			✓					✓	✻	✓	✓
Hilton (Disney Village)	✓(2)	✓		✓		✓				✓		✓					✓	✻	✓	✓
Holiday Inn (buena vista)	✓																	✻	✓	✓
Holiday Inn (UCF))	✓	✓		✓		✓			✓			✓				✻		✻		
Hyatt Regency (cypress)	✓	✓		✓	✓		✓	✓	✓			✓			✓		✓	✓	✓	✓
Marriott (int'l drive)	✓(3)	✓															✓	✻		
Marriott (orlando airport)	✓	✓		✓	✓	✓			✓			✓					✓			
Marriott (world center)	✓(3)	✓		✓			✓	✓	✓			✓			✓		✓	✓	✓	✓
Omni International	✓	✓				✓			✓			✓								
Peabody Orlando	✓	✓		✓	✓		✓	✓		✓		✓					✓	✻		
Penta	✓	✓		✓	✓	✓			✓			✓						✻		
Radisson Plaza	✓	✓		✓		✓			✓			✓								
Sheraton World Resort	✓(3)	✓				✓			✓			✓					✓	✻		
Sonesta Villa Resort	✓	✓		✓		✓			✓			✓								
Stouffer Orlando	✓	✓		✓	✓		✓	✓	✓			✓					✓	✻		

✗–available at a nearby location.
✻–local health club privileges.

	Pool	Whirlpool	Hot tub	Sauna	Steam room	Exercise equipment	Exercise room	Instructor	Weights	Weight machine	Stair machine	Stationary bicycle	Treadmill	Rowing machine	Jogging trail	Tennis	Lighted tennis courts	Golf	Putting green	Driving range
Disney Inn Resort ✻	✓(2)					✓				✓		✓					✓	✻		
The Enclave	✓(3)	✓		✓	✓	✓			✓			✓					✓	✻		
Twin Towers	✓	✓		✓		✓				✓				✓						
Vistana	✓(5)	✓		✓	✓	✓						✓			✓		✓			
Walt Disney Dolphin	✓(3)	✓					✓	✓		✓		✓					✓	✻		
Walt Disney Swan	✓(2)	✓		✓		✓				✓		✓					✓	✻		
PHILADELPHIA																				
Adam's Mark	✓	✓		✓			✓	✓	✓			✓								
Best Western	✓					✓				✓		✓								
Four Seasons	✓	✓		✓			✓	✓	✓			✓								
Guest Quarters	✓	✓		✓		✓			✓			✓								
Hilton & Towers	✓	✓		✓	✓		✓	✓	✓			✓								
Holiday Inn (bucks country)	✓	✓		✓	✓	✓			✓			✓								
Holiday Inn (center city)	✓					✓			✓			✓								
Hotel Atop the Bellevue ✻	✻	✓		✓																
Marriott (airport)	✓	✓		✓		✓			✓			✓								
Omni Hotel	✓	✓		✓		✓				✓		✓								
Radisson	✓	✓				✓				✓		✓								
Radnor	✓					✓				✓				✓						
Ramada	✓	✓		✓		✓			✓			✓								
Sheraton Inn ✻	✓					✓			✓			✓								
Sheraton (society hill)	✓	✓		✓			✓	✓	✓			✓								
The Rittenhouse	✓			✓			✓	✓		✓		✓								
Ritz-Carlton	✻			✓			✓	✓		✓		✓								
Wyndham	✓	✓		✓	✓		✓	✓	✓			✓	✓							
PITTSBURGH																				
Harley	✓(2)	✓		✓													✓			
Hilton				✓	✓	✓			✓			✓								
Hilton (airport inn)	✓					✓			✓			✓								
Hyatt Regency	✓	✓		✓	✓	✓			✓			✓								
Marriott	✓(2)	✓		✓		✓			✓			✓								
Marriott (greentree)	✓(3)	✓		✓	✓	✓				✓		✓				✻				
Sheraton	✓	✓				✓			✓			✓								

✗–available at a nearby location.
✱–local facility privileges.

	Pool	Whirlpool	Hot tub	Sauna	Steam room	Exercise equipment	Exercise room	Instructor	Weights	Weight machine	Stair machine	Stationary bicycle	Treadmill	Rowing machine	Jogging trail	Tennis	Lighted tennis courts	Golf	Putting green	Driving range
Vista	✓	✓		✓	✓		✓	✓	✓			✓								
Westin						✓						✓	✓							
PHOENIX																				
Best Western	✓	✓					✓	✓	✓			✓					✓	✱		
Courtyard	✓	✓				✓				✓		✓								
Crescent	✓	✓		✓	✓		✓	✓	✓			✓								
Crowne Sterling	✓	✓														✱		✱		
Doubletree ✱	✓	✓		✓												✓				
Fountain Suites	✓	✓		✓													✓	✱		
Hilton	✓	✓				✓				✓		✓								
Hyatt	✓	✓														✓				
Pointe Hilton	✓(6)	✓		✓	✓		✓	✓	✓			✓					✓	✓	✓	
Sheraton Greenway	✓																✓	✱		✓
Ritz-Carlton	✓	✓		✓			✓	✓		✓		✓					✓	✱		
PORTLAND, ME																				
Black Point Inn	✓(2)	✓		✓		✓						✓		✓		✱		✱		
Holiday Inn (by the bay)	✓			✓		✓						✓		✓		✱		✱		
Holiday Inn (west)	✓	✓		✓		✓					✓		✓							
Inn by the Sea	✓	✓															✓			
Marriott (sable oaks)	✓	✓		✓		✓			✓			✓								
Portland Regency		✓		✓			✓	✓	✓			✓								
Quality Suites		✓		✓		✓				✓		✓								
Sheraton Tara	✓			✓			✓	✓		✓		✓								
Sonesta				✓		✓				✓			✓							
PORTLAND, OR																				
Best Western (pony sodier)	✓	✓		✓		✓				✓		✓								
Embassy Suites ✱	✓	✓		✓		✓				✓		✓								
Hilton	✓					✓			✓				✓							
Holiday Inn (airport)	✓	✓		✓		✓			✓			✓								
Howard Jonson	✓	✓		✓		✓				✓		✓								
Marriott	✓	✓		✓		✓								✓						
Sheraton (airport)	✓	✓		✓		✓			✓			✓								

✗–available at a nearby location.
✱–local facility privileges.

	Pool	Whirlpool	Hot tub	Sauna	Steam room	Exercise equipment	Exercise room	Instructor	Weights	Weight machine	Stair machine	Stationary bicycle	Treadmill	Rowing machine	Jogging trail	Tennis	Lighted tennis courts	Golf	Putting green	Driving range
PROVIDENCE																				
Holiday Inn ✱	✓	✓																		
Marriott	✓	✓		✓		✓			✓			✓								
Ramada Inn	✓	✓		✓												✓		✱		
RALEIGH																				
Courtyard	✓	✓				✓			✓			✓								
Embassy Suites	✓	✓		✓	✓	✓				✓			✓							
Hilton	✓	✓				✓				✓		✓								
Marriott Crabtree	✓	✓				✓				✓		✓								
RAPID CITY																				
Hilton Inn	✓	✓				✓						✓		✓						
Holiday Inn	✓	✓		✓		✓				✓		✓								
Howard Johnson	✓	✓		✓	✓	✓			✓			✓								
RICHMOND, VA																				
Commonwealth Park		✓		✓		✓						✓	✓							
Courtyard	✓	✓				✓				✓		✓								
Embassy Suites	✓	✓		✓	✓	✓				✓		✓								
Hilton (airport)	✓	✓				✓				✓		✓								
Hyatt	✓	✓		✓		✓				✓	✓						✓			
Marriott	✓	✓		✓		✓			✓			✓								
Omni	✓	✓		✓	✓		✓	✓	✓											
Radisson	✓	✓				✓			✓			✓								
Sheraton Inn (airport)	✓	✓		✓	✓	✓			✓			✓								
ST. LOUIS																				
Adam's Mark	✓(2)	✓					✓	✓		✓		✓								
Cheshire Inn	✓	✓		✓	✓		✓	✓	✓			✓								
Courtyard	✓	✓				✓			✓			✓								
Doubletree (conf. ctr.)	✓(2)	✓		✓	✓		✓	✓	✓			✓					✓			
Doubletree (mayfair)	✓					✓				✓		✓								
Frontenac Grand	✓	✓		✓		✓			✓			✓								
Henry VIII	✓(2)	✓		✓		✓			✓	✓							✓			
Hilton	✓	✓		✓		✓			✓			✓								
Holiday Inn (airport)	✓	✓		✓		✓			✓			✓								

✗–available at a nearby location.
✱–local facility privileges.

	Pool	Whirlpool	Hot tub	Sauna	Steam room	Exercise equipment	Exercise room	Instructor	Weights	Weight machine	Stair machine	Stationary bicycle	Treadmill	Rowing machine	Jogging trail	Tennis	Lighted tennis courts	Golf	Putting green	Driving range
Hyatt (union station)	✓					✓				✓		✓								
Marriott	✓(2)	✓		✓			✓	✓	✓			✓					✓			
Marriott Pavilion	✓	✓		✓		✓			✓			✓								
Marriott West	✓(2)	✓		✓		✓			✓			✓								
Radisson	✓(2)	✓		✓	✓	✓			✓			✓								
Radisson (airport)	✓	✓				✓				✓		✓								
Sheraton Plaza ✱	✓	✓		✓												✱				
Sheraton Westport ✱	✓															✱				
Stouffer	✓(2)	✓		✓		✓			✓			✓								
Ritz-Carlton	✓	✓		✓			✓	✓		✓		✓								
SALT LAKE CITY																				
Clarion	✓	✓		✓		✓				✓		✓				✓			✓	
Doubletree	✓	✓		✓		✓				✓		✓								
Embassy Suites	✓	✓		✓		✓					✓	✓								
Hilton	✓	✓		✓		✓				✓		✓								
Little America	✓(2)	✓		✓		✓			✓			✓								
Marriott	✓	✓		✓		✓			✓			✓				✱				
Peery		✓				✓				✓		✓								
Radisson (airport)	✓					✓					✓	✓								
Red Lion	✓	✓		✓		✓			✓			✓								
University Park	✓	✓				✓				✓		✓				✱				
SAN FRANCISCO																				
Crown Sterling (south)✱	✓	✓		✓		✓				✓		✓								
Crown Sterling (airport)✱	✓	✓		✓	✓														✓	
Hilton	✓	✓		✓	✓	✓			✓			✓								
Hilton (airport)	✓	✓				✓			✓			✓								
Holiday Inn (crowne plaza)	✓	✓		✓		✓			✓			✓								
Hyatt (airport)	✓	✓		✓		✓				✓		✓								
Marriott (moscone)	✓	✓		✓		✓				✓		✓								
Marriott (airport)	✓	✓		✓		✓			✓			✓								
Sheraton Palace	✓	✓		✓		✓			✓				✓							
Ritz-Carlton	✓	✓		✓																
Westin (airport)	✓	✓		✓		✓				✓		✓								

✗–available at a nearby location.
✱–local facility privileges.

	Pool	Whirlpool	Hot tub	Sauna	Steam room	Exercise equipment	Exercise room	Instructor	Weights	Weight machine	Stair machine	Stationary bicycle	Treadmill	Rowing machine	Jogging trail	Tennis	Lighted tennis courts	Golf	Putting green	Driving range
SEATTLE																				
Best Western	✓	✓		✓	✓	✓			✓			✓								
Doubletree	✓	✓		✓		✓			✓			✓								
Four Seasons	✓	✓		✓			✓	✓	✓			✓				✱				
Hilton ✱	✓	✓		✓																
Hilton (airport)	✓	✓				✓			✓			✓								
Holiday Inn (crowne plaza)	✓	✓		✓		✓			✓			✓								
Holiday Inn (airport)	✓	✓				✓			✓			✓								
Marriott (airport)	✓	✓		✓		✓			✓			✓								
Radisson (airport)	✓			✓		✓			✓			✓								
Sheraton Hotel	✓	✓		✓			✓	✓	✓			✓								
Stouffer (madison)	✓	✓				✓			✓			✓								
Westin	✓	✓		✓			✓	✓	✓			✓								
TALLAHASSEE																				
Courtyard	✓	✓				✓				✓		✓								
Radisson				✓		✓			✓			✓								
TUCSON																				
Arizona Inn	✓																✓	✱		
Best Western (catalina)	✓	✓				✓				✓		✓								
Best Western (royal sun)	✓	✓		✓		✓				✓		✓								
Clarion ✱	✓	✓																✱		
Courtyard	✓	✓				✓				✓		✓								
Doubletree	✓	✓				✓				✓		✓					✓			
Embassy Suites	✓	✓				✓				✓		✓								
Hilton & Towers ✱	✓	✓				✓			✓		✓					✱		✱		
Holiday Inn (pablo verde)	✓	✓		✓		✓			✓			✓					✓			
Hotel Parc Tucson ✱	✓															✱		✱		
Loew's Ventana	✓	✓		✓	✓		✓	✓		✓		✓					✓	✓	✓	✓
Ramada Inn (airport)	✓	✓				✓				✓		✓								
Sheraton	✓	✓		✓			✓	✓	✓			✓					✓	✓	✓	✓
Tucson Nat'l Resort	✓	✓		✓	✓		✓	✓	✓			✓					✓	✓	✓	✓
Ventana Canyon	✓	✓		✓	✓		✓	✓		✓		✓					✓	✓	✓	✓
Westin	✓	✓					✓	✓		✓		✓					✓	✓	✓	✓

✗–available at a nearby location.
✱–local facility privileges.

	Pool	Whirlpool	Hot tub	Sauna	Steam room	Exercise equipment	Exercise room	Instructor	Weights	Weight machine	Stair machine	Stationary bicycle	Treadmill	Rowing machine	Jogging trail	Tennis	Lighted tennis courts	Golf	Putting green	Driving range
WASHINGTON D.C.																				
Ana	✓	✓		✓	✓	✓				✓		✓								
Courtyard	✓	✓				✓			✓			✓								
Courtyard (fair oaks)	✓	✓				✓			✓			✓								
Embassy Suites	✓	✓				✓						✓		✓						
Embassy (crystal city)	✓					✓				✓		✓								
Four Seasons	✓						✓	✓		✓		✓								
Grand	✓	✓				✓				✓		✓								
Grand Hyatt	✓	✓		✓	✓	✓			✓			✓								
Hilton (tysons corner)	✓			✓			✓	✓	✓			✓								
Holiday Inn (crowne plaza)	✓	✓		✓			✓	✓	✓			✓								
Howard Johnson						✓			✓			✓								
Hyatt (arlington)						✓						✓	✓							
Hyatt (dulles)	✓	✓		✓		✓			✓			✓								
Hyatt (fair lakes)	✓	✓		✓		✓			✓			✓								
Hyatt	✓			✓		✓						✓		✓						
Hyatt (crystal city)	✓	✓		✓		✓				✓	✓									
Hyatt (reston town center)	✓	✓		✓			✓	✓	✓			✓				✱		✱		
J.W. Marriott	✓	✓		✓			✓	✓	✓			✓								
Loew's Marriott	✓						✓	✓	✓			✓								
Marriott	✓(2)	✓		✓			✓	✓	✓			✓					✓			
Marriott (crystal gateway)	✓	✓		✓		✓			✓			✓				✱				
Marriott (greenbelt)	✓(2)	✓		✓		✓			✓			✓					✓			
Marriott (key bridge)	✓	✓		✓		✓			✓			✓								
Marriott Suites	✓	✓				✓			✓			✓								
Marriott (crystal city)	✓	✓		✓		✓			✓			✓								
Marriott (tysons corner)	✓	✓		✓		✓			✓					✓						
Park Hyatt	✓	✓		✓	✓		✓	✓		✓		✓				✱		✱		
Ramada (renaissance)	✓	✓		✓			✓	✓		✓		✓								
Ranada (tysons corner)	✓	✓		✓		✓			✓			✓								
Renaissance	✓	✓				✓			✓				✓							
Sheraton (crystal city)	✓			✓		✓			✓			✓								
Sheraton (national)	✓			✓		✓				✓		✓								

✗–available at a nearby location.
✱–local facility privileges.

	Pool	Whirlpool	Hot tub	Sauna	Steam room	Exercise equipment	Exercise room	Instructor	Weights	Weight machine	Stair machine	Stationary bicycle	Treadmill	Rowing machine	Jogging trail	Tennis	Lighted tennis courts	Golf	Putting green	Driving range
Sheraton (premier)	✓(2)	✓		✓			✓	✓	✓			✓					✱	✱		
Sheraton (reston)	✓			✓		✓				✓				✓			✓			
Stouffer (concourse)	✓	✓		✓		✓				✓		✓				✱				
Stouffer (mayflower) ✱						✓				✓		✓								
The Capital Hilton				✓	✓	✓			✓			✓								
The Carlton	✱					✓						✓	✓			✱		✱		
Ritz-Carlton ✱																✱		✱		
Ritz-Carlton (pentagon city)	✓	✓		✓			✓	✓		✓		✓				✱		✱		
Ritz-Carlton (tysons corner)	✓	✓		✓			✓	✓		✓		✓				✱		✱		
Washington Court				✓		✓				✓		✓								
Washington Vista				✓		✓			✓			✓								
Watergate	✓	✓		✓	✓		✓	✓		✓		✓								
Willard (inter-continental) ✱	✱					✓			✓			✓								
Woodfin Suites	✓			✓		✓				✓			✓							
WHEELING, WV																				
Oglebay's (wilson lodge)	✓(2)	✓															✓	✓		✓
WILMINGTON																				
Marriott Suites ✱	✓			✓		✓				✓		✓								
Radisson	✓	✓				✓			✓			✓								
CANADA																				
CALGARY																				
Best Western (kananaskis)	✓	✓			✓													✓		
Blackfoot Inn	✓	✓		✓		✓						✓		✓				✱		
Chateau (airport)	✓	✓		✓		✓			✓			✓								
Delta Bow Valley	✓	✓		✓		✓			✓			✓								
Hotel Kananaskis	✓	✓		✓		✓			✓				✓			✓		✓	✓	✓
International	✓	✓		✓		✓			✓			✓								
Lodge at Kananaskis	✓	✓		✓	✓	✓			✓				✓			✓		✓	✓	✓
Palliser						✓			✓			✓								
Sheraton Cavalier	✓	✓		✓																
Skyline Plaza ✱	✓	✓		✓		✓						✓		✓						
Westin	✓	✓		✓		✓			✓			✓								

✗–available at a nearby location.
✱–local facility privileges.

	Pool	Whirlpool	Hot tub	Sauna	Steam room	Exercise equipment	Exercise room	Instructor	Weights	Weight machine	Stair machine	Stationary bicycle	Treadmill	Rowing machine	Jogging trail	Tennis	Lighted tennis courts	Golf	Putting green	Driving range
MONTREAL																				
Delta	✓(2)	✓		✓			✓	✓	✓			✓								
Holiday Inn (crowne plaza)	✓	✓		✓		✓			✓			✓								
Holiday Inn (conv. center)	✓						✓	✓		✓		✓								
Hostellerie Les Trois	✓	✓															✓	✗		
Hostellerie Rive Gauche	✓																✓	✗		
Howard Johnson (plaza)				✓		✓			✓			✓								
Inter-Continental	✓						✓	✓		✓			✓							
La Citadelle	✓			✓	✓	✓				✓										
Le Centre Sheraton	✓	✓		✓	✓		✓	✓	✓			✓								
Le Chateau Champlain	✓	✓		✓			✓	✓	✓			✓								
Le Chateau Montebello	✓(2)	✓		✓			✓	✓		✓		✓				✓		✓	✓	
Le Meridien	✓	✓		✓																
Le Pavillon	✓	✓		✓																
Le Quatre Saisons	✓	✓		✓	✓		✓	✓	✓			✓								
OTTAWA																				
Albert at Bay		✓		✓		✓				✓		✓								
Chateau Laurier	✓			✓																
Delta	✓			✓		✓			✓			✓								
Hilton	✓	✓		✓		✓			✓			✓								
Plaza de la Chaudiere	✓	✓		✓												✱				
Radisson (ottowa center)	✓	✓		✓			✓	✓	✓			✓								
Westin	✓	✓	✓	✓			✓	✓	✓			✓								
TORONTO																				
Delta Chelsea Inn	✓(2)	✓		✓		✓			✓			✓								
Four Seasons	✓	✓		✓	✓	✓			✓			✓								
Guild	✓					✓				✓		✓					✓			
Hilton International	✓	✓		✓		✓			✓			✓								
Holiday Inn on King	✓			✓		✓				✓				✓						
Howard Johnson (east)	✓	✓		✓		✓			✓			✓								
Howard Johnson (plaza)						✓			✓			✓								
Inn on the Park	✓(2)	✓		✓	✓	✓			✓			✓					✓			
Inter-Continental	✓			✓		✓			✓				✓							

✗–available at a nearby location.
✱–local facility privileges.

	Pool	Whirlpool	Hot tub	Sauna	Steam room	Exercise equipment	Exercise room	Instructor	Weights	Weight machine	Stair machine	Stationary bicycle	Treadmill	Rowing machine	Jogging trail	Tennis	Lighted tennis courts	Golf	Putting green	Driving range
King Edward		✓		✓		✓			✓			✓								
L'Hotel	✓	✓		✓		✓			✓			✓								
Marriott (airport)	✓	✓		✓			✓	✓	✓			✓								
Millcraft	✓	✓		✓		✓			✓			✓				✓		✱		
Novotel Centre	✓	✓		✓		✓			✓					✓						
Radisson (airport)	✱					✓			✓			✓								
Radisson (don valley)	✓	✓		✓	✓	✓			✓			✓								
Ramada (don valley) ✱	✓			✓																
Regal Constellation	✓	✓		✓		✓			✓			✓								
Royal York	✓	✓		✓		✓				✓				✓						
Sheraton Centre	✓	✓		✓		✓			✓			✓								
Sheraton (east)	✓	✓		✓		✓			✓			✓								
Sutton Place	✓	✓		✓		✓			✓			✓								
Swissotel (airport)	✓	✓		✓		✓			✓					✓						
The Bristol Place	✓			✓		✓			✓			✓								
Valhalla Inn	✓	✓		✓		✓				✓			✓							
Westin Harbour	✓	✓		✓	✓		✓	✓	✓			✓				✓				
WINNIPEG																				
Best Western (Int'l)	✓(2)	✓		✓																
Birchwood Inn	✓	✓		✓		✓			✓			✓								
Delta	✓	✓				✓			✓					✓						
Holiday Inn (crowne plaza)	✓(2)	✓		✓			✓	✓	✓			✓								
Sheraton ✱	✓	✓		✓																
Westin	✓	✓		✓		✓			✓			✓								
VANCOUVER																				
Coast Plaza	✓			✓	✓		✓	✓	✓			✓								
Delta Pacific	✓(3)	✓		✓			✓	✓	✓			✓								
Delta Place	✓	✓					✓	✓	✓			✓								
Executive Inn ✱	✓	✓																		
Four Seasons	✓	✓		✓			✓	✓	✓			✓				✱				
Georgian Court		✓		✓		✓			✓			✓								
Hotel Vancouver	✓	✓		✓			✓	✓	✓			✓								
Meridien	✓	✓		✓	✓		✓	✓	✓			✓								

RESOURCE LIST

2 *Travel Holiday* (June 1993), 28 West 23rd St., New York, NY 10010.

3 Courtesy *Condé Nast Traveler.* Copyright © 1993 by The Condé Nast Publications Inc.

8 *Condé Nast Traveler.* Copyright © 1993.

9 Heyman, Tom. *In An Average Lifetime;* Ballantine Books, a division of Random House, Inc., New York: 1991.

11 Warshaw, Hope S., M.M.Sc., R.D. *The Healthy Eater's Guide to Family & Chain Restaurants;* CHRONIMED Publishing, Minneapolis: 1993.

12 *Traveling Healthy,* 108-48 70th Road, Forest Hills, NY 11375. Reprinted with permission.

18 Welch, Thomas G., M.D. *Minute Health Tips;* CHRONIMED Publishing, Minneapolis: 1991.

19 *The Healthy Eater's Guide to Family & Chain Restaurants:* 1993.

21 *Traveling Healthy.*

22 First appeared in *Working Woman* in February 1993. Written by Catherine Fredman. Reprinted with the permission of *Working Woman* magazine. Copyright © 1993 by *Working Woman* Magazine.

25 *Travel Holiday* (July/August 1993).

35 *Restaurant Hospitality*, 1100 Superior Avenue, Cleveland, OH 44114. Reprinted with permission.

38 Krantz, Les. *America By The Numbers;* Houghton Mifflin Company, New York: 1993.

39 Reprinted with permission from *Entrepreneur* Magazine, December 1992.

47 *Restaurant Hospitality.*

53 First appeared in *Working Woman* in July 1993. Written by Laurie Kretchmar. Reprinted with the permission of *Working Woman* magazine. Copyright © 1993 by *Working Woman* Magazine.

54 Reprinted from *Men's Health* Magazine. Copyright 1993 Rodale Press, Inc. All rights reserved.

55 *Traveling Healthy.*

56 *In An Average Lifetime:* 1991.

57 Reprinted from *Men's Health* Magazine. Copyright 1993 Rodale Press, Inc. All rights reserved.

59 *Traveling Healthy.*

61 First appeared in *Working Woman* in July 1993. Written by Laurie Kretchmar. Reprinted with the permission of *Working Woman* magazine. Copyright © 1993 by *Working Woman* Magazine.

62 *Traveling Healthy.*

64 Reprinted from *Men's Health* Magazine. Copyright 1993 Rodale Press, Inc. All rights reserved.

65 *Travel Holiday* (July/August 1993).

69 Reprinted with permission from *Psychology Today,* Copyright © 1993 (Sussex Publishers, Inc.).

79 *Traveling Healthy.*

80 *America By The Numbers*: 1993.

81 *Minute Health Tips:* 1991.

91 *Traveling Healthy.*

103 *Traveling Healthy.*

106 *Traveling Healthy.*

109 *Traveling Healthy.*

114 *In An Average Lifetime:* 1991.

115 Panati, Charles. *The Browser's Book of Beginnings;* Houghton Mifflin Company, New York: 1984.

125 *Minute Health Tips:* 1991.

127 *The Diabetic Traveler,* P.O. Box 8223, Stamford, CT 06905.

133 *FDA Consumer* (October, 1993), 5600 Fishers Lane, Room 15A-19, Rockville, MD 20857.

144 *Sales & Marketing Management* (June 1993), Bill Communications, 355 Park Avenue South, New York, NY 10010-1789.

145 *Psychology Today.* © 1993.

147 *Sales & Marketing Management* (June 1993).

149 *Traveling Healthy.*

151 *Condé Nast Traveler.* Copyright © 1993.

153 *Sales & Marketing Management* (April 1993).

154 *Traveling Healthy.*

155 Reprinted with permission © *American Demographics,* (July 1993). For subscription information, please call (800) 828-1133.

157 *America By The Numbers*: 1993.

163 *Traveling Healthy.*

INDEX

BOOKS OF RELATED INTEREST

Convenience Food Facts by Arlene Monk, R.D., C.D.E., with an introduction by Marion Franz, R.D., M.S. Includes complete nutrition information, tips, and exchange values on more than 1,500 popular name brand processed foods commonly found in grocery store freezers and shelves. Helps you plan easy-to-prepare, nutritious meals. ☐

004081 ISBN 0-937721-77-8 $10.95

Fast Food Facts by Marion Franz, R.D., M.S. This revised and up-to-date best-seller shows how to make smart nutrition choices at fast food restaurants–and tells what to avoid. Includes complete nutrition information on more than 1,000 menu offerings from the 21 largest fast food chains.

Standard-size edition 004068 ISBN 0-937721-67-0 $6.95 ☐

Pocket edition 004073 ISBN 0-937721-69-7 $4.95 ☐

The Healthy Eater's Guide to Family & Chain Restaurants by Hope S. Warshaw, M.M.Sc., R.D. Here's the only guide that tells you how to eat healthier in over 100 of America's most popular family and chain restaurants. It offers complete and up-to-date nutrition information and suggests which items to choose and avoid. ☐

004214 ISBN 1-56561-017-2 $9.95

Exchanges for All Occasions by Marion Franz, R.D., M.S. Exchanges and meal planning suggestions for just about any occasion, sample meal plans, special tips for people with diabetes, and more. ☐

004201 ISBN 1-56561-005-9 $12.95

The Brand Name Pocket Guide to Additive-Free Foods by J. Michael Lapchick with Rosa A. Mo, R.D., Ed.D, is the first quick reference to over 1000 brand name products that are free from preservatives, artificial sweeteners, colors or flavors, and any other synthetic additives. You'll find most of the foods you already eat–complete with calorie, fat, cholesterol, sodium, carbohydrate, and exchange breakdowns. ☐

004237 ISBN 1-56561-040-7 $9.95

Emergency Medical Treatment: Infants, Children, Adults: Revised and Expanded Edition by Stephen Vogel, M.D., and David Manhoff, produced in cooperation with the National Safety Council. With over 1.5 million copies sold, the #1–selling guide of its kind has saved countless lives and is now totally updated with the newest safety guidelines. Written especially for people untrained in emergency medical procedures, this indispensable, step-by-step guide tells exactly what to do during the most common, life-threatening situations you might encounter for infants, children, and adults.

004627 ISBN 0-916363-10-4 $12.95

Fight Fat & Win by Elaine Moquette-Magee, R.D., M.P.H. This breakthrough book explains how to easily incorporate low-fat dietary guidelines into every modern eating experience, from fastfood and common restaurants to quick meals at home, simply by making smarter choices. ☐

004070 ISBN 0-937721-65-4 $9.95